WITHDRAWAL

A BIBLIOGRAPHY
OF THE RESTORATION DRAMA

A Bibliography

of the

Restoration Drama

by

Montague Summers

*" From 1660 down to 1710 nothing in dramatic
form comes amiss."*

EDMUND GOSSE.

NEW YORK / RUSSELL & RUSSELL

FIRST PUBLISHED IN 1934
REISSUED, 1970, BY RUSSELL & RUSSELL
A DIVISION OF ATHENEUM PUBLISHERS, INC.
L. C. CATALOG CARD NO: 70-81479
PRINTED IN THE UNITED STATES OF AMERICA

INTRODUCTION

THE plan of the following Bibliography is to supply, as far as our present knowledge extends, a complete list of all plays, acted and unacted, printed and unprinted, belonging to the Restoration Theatre, a dramatic period which is commonly taken to cover the years from the general re-opening of the public playhouses (1660) to the death of Dryden, in 1700. It is, of course, inevitable that such convenient and accepted terms as " Restoration period " or " Restoration Theatre " should be very flexible in their connotation. It were impossible in any account of the Restoration stage, historical, critical or bibliographical, to ignore the earlier work of such men as Davenant, Killigrew, or even the Duke of Newcastle and Thomas Jordan, who were writing in the reign of Charles I, and whose activities during the interregnum are of essential importance. On the other hand, Sir John Vanbrugh and Farquhar must certainly (for our purpose, at any rate) be accounted Restoration dramatists, and a student who, on consulting the Bibliography, found that in the case of the former nothing was set down after *The Pilgrim*, and in the case of the latter only *Love and a Bottle* and *The Constant Couple* were recorded, would have very just and legitimate cause for complaint.

A serious difficulty arises in dealing with Colley Cibber, whose first four plays in point of time fall within the period, but of whom over twenty plays, including his most famous comedies, belong to the eighteenth century. Not only were such pieces as *The Careless Husband*, *The Non-Juror*, and *The Provok'd Husband* produced in the reigns of Queen Anne, George I, and George II respectively, but both in fashion, in sentiment, in atmosphere and in moral these comedies are Non-Restoration and entirely typical of their own day. The bibliography of *The Provok'd Husband*, which kept the London stage until the fifteenth season of Phelps, 1858–59, and was seen even more recently in the provinces, is elaborate and immense. Not only so, but as it appears in later reprints—for example, Oxberry's Edition, 1819—whole episodes are omitted, scenes are transposed, dialogue is jettisoned, characters are shuffled, and to give (without some cautel at least) this badly-cut nineteenth-century prompt book in a Bibliography of Restoration Drama were surely impertinent and intrusive.

Such an *omnium gatherum* is beside the present design. This Bibliography aims at listing all editions of contemporary plays published between the years 1660 and 1700; all editions, indeed, that appeared during a writer's lifetime, and therefore may justly be considered of some authority. I have not judged it necessary to record in every instance the inclusion of a play in the many eighteenth and nineteenth-century Collections, such as *The New English Theatre*, 1776; *Bell's British Theatre*, 1792; John Sharpe's *British Theatre*, 1805; Mrs. Inchbald's *British Theatre*, 1808; Sir Walter Scott's *Modern British Drama*, 1811; R. Cumberland's *British Drama*, 1817; *The Select London Stage*, 4 vols., 1824, and one vol., no date (1824); John Cumberland's *British Theatre*, 1829 and following years; Lacy; John Dicks.

The reason why I have eschewed the by-ways of these Collections in detail is not far to seek. A student will require an unadulterated and original text, and any reference to these eighteenth-century reprints might very easily become a fruitful source of error. Thus Dryden's *Amphitryon* as reprinted, 8vo, 1777, "For T. Lowndes, T. Caslon, C. Corbett, and S. Bladon," is not only given as "Altered from Dryden, by Mr. Woodward," but also as "Marked with the Variations of the Manager's Book, at the Theatre-Royal in Covent-Garden." In this edition the play was sold separately at sixpence, and was also included in *The New English Theatre*, Vol. IX, with general title-page, 1777. When reprinted, 12mo, 1792, for John Bell, *Amphitryon* was presented "As Altered from Dryden by Dr. Hawkesworth. Adapted for Theatrical Representation"; and, as if this were not enough, it was "Regulated from the Prompt-Books, *By Permission of the Managers*," of the Theatres Royal, Drury Lane and Covent Garden. Even so there are a great many lines, including some of the wittiest passages in the play, distinguished by inverted commas, and omitted in the Representation.

In 1777 Southerne's *The Fatal Marriage; or, The Innocent Adultery*, was reprinted "for C. Bathurst; T. Lowndes; T. Longman; T. Caslon; W. Nicoll; S. Bladon, and Wheildon and Co.," as *Isabella; or, The Fatal Marriage*, "A Tragedy, *Altered from* Southern, By D. Garrick, Esq. Marked with the Variations in the Manager's Book, At The Theatre-Royal in Drury-Lane." Price 6*d*. This was included in *The New English Theatre*, Vol. XII, with general title-page, 1777. In R. Cumberland's *The British Drama*, Vol. I, 1817, we have *Isabella; or The Fatal Marriage*, "Altered from Southern. Adapted for Theatrical Representation, *As performed at the Theatres-Royal*, Covent-Garden and Drury-Lane. Regulated from the Prompt Books, By Permission of the Managers. . . . The lines distinguished by inverted Commas are omitted in the Representation. Cooke's Edition." In his *Critique*

Cumberland, p. x, informs us that "Southern has mingled so much dross with his gold, that it has been necessary to refine it over and over again."

After *Amphitryon* and *The Fatal Marriage* (which latter, perhaps, fared the worse) had been thus boultered through half-a-dozen sieves of adapters, recensors, managers, prompters, regulators and the rest, there is very little left of the originals, and it were not merely superfluous, it were actually mischievous, to record in a bibliography all these caponizings and mutilations.

There is, to my knowledge, no Bibliography of the Restoration Drama, and it seems obvious from the great awakening of interest in the theatre of Charles II and his immediate successors that such a work of reference has long been badly needed. In the present Bibliography my design, then, has been to give under the authors' names, which are arranged in alphabetical order, and in sequence of production on the stage the plays, printed and unprinted, that each dramatist has written. In the case of published work I record the first edition and all following editions that appeared during the writer's lifetime. In the majority of instances I have added a list of all important subsequent reprints but for the reasons which I have just explained in some detail I thought it undesirable to make this list exhaustive in the strict sense of the word, since this would necessitate the tabulation of unsound and imperfect material. Yet I have not (I think) omitted any reprint which possesses features (however few) of value or consequence.

Recent editions, as being the most readily accessible, I have been careful to catalogue, and less critically, but the appearance of a modern reprint in this list must not necessarily be taken to imply any specific recommendation.

Where, as has sometimes happened of late, the issue of a standard edition of a dramatist was followed by a number of cheap and derivative reprints I have judged it improper to draw attention to these parasites, and if the student (as well as the more general reader) is for some reason not able to avail himself of the recognized edition he will do best to fall back upon the Mermaid texts, that is to say, in such instances as when an author is to be found in this admirable series, although I regret to observe that this holds good in only three cases of Restoration dramatists. If the reader will bear in mind that the Mermaid text has been modernized in arrangement, not unseldom to the disruption of the original technique, he will with this one salvo soon be deeply beholden to these eminently readable books, and he will be well advised to study closely the Introductions furnished by such men as John Addington Symonds, Edmund Gosse, Arthur Symons and Havelock Ellis. I speak of the Mermaid Series, under the general editorship of Dr. Havelock Ellis. The volumes issued after it had passed from his care are hardly to be approved.

In the case of each acted play I have recorded the original date of production, and the house at which it was given. So far as possible I make it my object to avoid that most irritating word *circa*, yet I fear in some few instances it became inevitable, since data were so entirely lacking.

Such notes as I have appended, although, I hope, sufficient, are of the briefest. I felt that it was no part of a bibliographer to set up critical sea-marks, and therefore I scrupulously refrain from any comment upon certain modern reprints, which I frankly confess to having admitted with the greatest hesitation.

The upright strokes by which the alignment of wording upon the title-pages of books is designated I have decided to disregard, save in only one instance, the Second Part of Dryden's *The Conquest of Granada*, 4to, 1672. This technnical manerism goes far to impair, even if it does not completely destroy, the readability of a book, and in the present Bibliography I am setting out to stress and emphasize the literary side of the Restoration Theatre, to chronicle the advent of a play upon the stage rather than aiming at equipping the collector with a manual of issues, states and sizes.

The first section records *Anonymous and Doubtful Plays*, under which I include a number of manuscripts which have not (I believe) been noticed before save in some instances (by no means all) in the catalogues of the great libraries where they are preserved. Several of these manuscripts, being in private hands, have not hitherto been in any way recorded. I do not think anyone will quarrel with me for mentioning the *Ternary of English Plays*, since 1662 is the date of the first printing of this leash, although of course *Grim, the Collier of Croydon*, is much earlier, and by many identified with William Haughton's *The Devil and his Dame*, for which see Henslowe's *Diary*, March, 1600.

I have employed the following abbreviations throughout the Bibliography : D.L., the Theatre Royal, Bridges Street, hard by Drury Lane. (I am, of course, aware that the term " Drury Lane " was not generally applied to the Theatre Royal until the end of the seventeenth century. See my *Restoration Theatre*, pp. 14–16 ; but I conceive that with this explanation the contraction D.L. is permissible). L.I.F., the Duke's Theatre, Lincoln's Inn Fields ; D.G., the Duke's Theatre, Dorset Garden. T.C., *The Term Catalogues*, edited by Edward Arber, 3 vols., 1903. S.R., *The Stationers' Register*.

A BIBLIOGRAPHY
OF THE RESTORATION DRAMA

ANONYMOUS AND DOUBTFUL PLAYS

A Phanatique Play. The First Part, As it was presented before and by the Lord *Fleetwood*, Sir *Arthur Hasilrig*, Sir *Henry Vane*, the Lord *Lambert* and others, last night, With Master *Iester* and Master *Pudding*. (This is the First Edition.) 4to. 1660. Unacted. (Another issue has, *A Phanatick Play*.)

A Parly Between The Ghosts Of The Late Protector And The King of Sweden, At their Meeting in Hell. 4to. London. Printed for Lo. Whimbleton. 1660. A political pamphlet, partly in dialogue. B.M. copy; 3 May. Unacted.

The Tragical Actors Or The Martyrdome of the late King Charles. Wherein *Oliver*'s late falsehood, with the rest of his gang are described in their several actions and stations. Unacted. 4to. The title-page carries no date, but the colophon runs, *Printed for Sir Arthur*. 1660.

Cromwell's Conspiracy. A Tragy-Comedy, Relating to our latter Times. Beginning at the Death of King Charles the First, And ending with the happy Restauration of King Charles the Second. Written by a Person of Quality. Unacted. 4to. 1660.

Love's Mystery. Not printed. Vere Street, 12th November, 1660.

Hells Higher Court of Justice; or the Triall of the Three Politick Ghosts, Viz. Oliver Cromwell, King of Sweden, and Cardinal Mazarine. Unacted. 4to. 1661 (13th April). Mazarin died 9th March, 1661.

Love's Quarrell. Salisbury Court, Saturday, 6th April, 1661. Not printed. (Pepys.)

Hewson Reduc'd : or, the Shoomaker return'd to his Trade. Unacted. 4to. 1661.

Andronicus : a Tragedy, Impieties Long Successe, or Heavens Late Revenge. 12mo. 1661. Unacted.

The Lyar. Vere Street, 1661. 4to. 1661. Revived at D.L. in the autumn of 1684, and printed, 4to, 1685, as *The Mistaken Beauty; Or, The Lyar.* From Corneille, *Le Menteur.*

The Dancing Master. Vere Street, 10th December, 1661. Otherwise *The Varietie.* See CAVENDISH, p. 35.

The History of Lewis XI, King of France. A Tragi-Comedy. Advertised at the end of *Wit and Drollery,* 12mo, 1661, as then printing, but never published.

Gratiæ Theatrales, or, A Choice Ternary of English Plays, viz. *Thorny-Abbey, or, The London-Maid,* a Tragedy by T. W. ; *The Marriage-Broker, or, The Pander,* a Comedy by M. W., M.A. ; *Grim the Collier of Croydon,* a comedy by I.T. 12mo. 1662.

The Faithfull Virgins. L.I.F. Date uncertain, but licensed by Herbert, and acted between 1661 and June, 1663 ; probably early in 1663. Bodley, Rawl. MSS. poet. 195.

The Unfortunate Usurper. A Tragedy. 4to. 1663. Unacted.

The Exposure. A pastoral. Theatre Royal, Bridges Street ; November, 1663 (Herbert). Not printed.

School Play. An Interlude. 8vo. 1664. Five scenes written for and performed in a private grammar-school in Middlesex in 1663.

Heraclius : A Tragedy. L.I.F. 8th March, 1664. (Pepys).

The Labyrinth, seen by Pepys at the Theatre Royal on 2nd May, 1664, is not printed. It does not appear that this was the same play as *The Labyrinth ; or, The Fatal Embarrassment,* a tragedy translated from Corneille ; Dublin, 8vo. 1795.

Irena, A Tragedy. Licensed, 13th October, 1664. Roger L' Estrange. 4to. 1664. Unacted.

Knavery in all Trades : or, The Coffee-House. A Comedy. As it was Acted in the Christmas Holidays by several Apprentices. 4to. 1664.

The Northerne Castle, seen by Pepys at the Theatre Royal on 14th September, 1667, is perhaps a mistake for Brome's *The Northern Lasse.*

The Poetess. D.L. October, 1667. Not printed.

The Feign'd Astrologer. Probably Lincoln's Inn Fields, 1668. 4to. 1668.

The Island Princess ; Or The Generous Portugal. D. L. 7th January, 1669. 4to. 1669. "With the Alterations and New Additional Scenes. Licensed May 31, 1669. Roger L'Estrange."

The Imperial Tragedy. Taken out of a Latin Play. And very much Altered By a Gentleman for his own Diversion. [Sir William Killigrew ?]. Folio, 1669. The Nursery.

Pluto Furens & Vinctus ; or The Raging Devil Bound. A Modern Farse. Per Philocomicum. Unacted. Amstedolami. 4to. 1669.

The Romantick Lady. D.L. March, 1671. Not printed.

The Religious-Rebell, Or The Pilgrim-Prince. A Tragedy. 4to. 1671. Unacted.

Emilia. London. Printed for the Author. A Trage-Comedy. 8vo. 1672. Unacted.

The Rectory. D.G. 27th September, 1673. Not printed.

The Sea-Captains. D.G. 18th March, 1674. Not printed.

Ballet et Musique pour le divertissement du Roy de la Grande Bretagne. 4to. 1674. "Dans la Savoye par Thomas Nieucombe."

The Armenian Queen. Duffett wrote for this play a Prologue and an Epilogue which are printed in his *New Poems, Songs, Prologues and Epilogues.* 8vo. 1676, pp. 84–87. *New Poems* is in the Term Catalogues for May,

1676, so probably *The Armenian Queen* was acted 1674–75. Nothing further is known of this play.

The Woman turn'd Bully. A Comedy. Dorset Garden about Easter (May), 1675. (S.R. 8th July, 1675). 4to. 1675. (T.C. Michaelmas, 24th November, 1675).

Piso's Conspiracy. A Tragedy. Dorset Garden autumn of 1675. 4to. 1676. (T.C. Hilary, 10th February, 1676).

No Fool like the Old Fool. D.L. June, 1676. Not printed.

The Lovers' Stratagem ; or, Virtue Rewarded. Not printed. Bodley, MS. Poet. Rawl. 18.

The Cyprian Conqueror; or, the faithless Relict. Not printed. B.M. Sloane MSS. 3709.

The Hypochondriac ; or, the turmoils of love. Not printed. B.M. Sloane MSS. 1863, ff.43b–70.

Iugurtha ; or, The Fait[h]less Cosen german. A Tragedy. Not printed. Bodley. Rawl. MSS. poet. 195.

The Captain ; or, The Town Miss. A Comedy. D.L. 2nd April, 1677. Not printed. Perhaps Fletcher's *The Captain.*

The Constant Nymph : Or The Rambling Shepheard. A Pastoral. Written by a Person of Quality. D.G. July, 1677. Licensed August the 13th. 1677. 4to. 1678.

The Counterfeit Bridegroom : Or The Defeated Widow. A Comedy. D.G. August, 1677. Licensed Octob. 4th, 1677. Robert L'Estrange. 4to. 1677. This alteration of Middleton's *No Wit, No Help like a Woman's* has been ascribed to Mrs. Behn, and also to Betterton. It is probably the work of the former.

The Polititian ; or, Sir Popular Wisdom. A Comedy. D.G. 17th November, 1677. Not printed. A satire on Shaftesbury.

The Cure of Pride, or, Every one in their Way. A Comedy,

extant MS., *c.* 1670–1680 (?). Not printed and not acted. An alteration of Massinger's *The City Madam.*

The Faithfull Genius. A Tragi-Comedy. Not printed, and not acted; extant MS.

The Coronation of Queen Elizabeth, With The Restauration Of The Protestant Religion: Or, The Downfal Of The Pope. Being a most Excellent Play As it was Acted Both at *Bartholomew* and *Southwark* Fairs This Present Year 1680 With Great Applause. 4to. 1680. The Bodleian Copy has a contemporary MS. note: "28th Sept." Bartholomew Fair at the Restoration was extended to fourteen days; and Southwark Fair, which originally had continued 7th, 8th, 9th September, was similarly prolonged.

The Muse of New-Market: or, Mirth and Drollery Being Three Farces Acted before the King and Court at New-Market; Viz. The Merry Milk-Maid of Islington, Or The Rambling Gallants defeated. Love lost in the Dark Or The Drunken Couple. The Politick Whore or the Conceited Cuckhold. 4to. 1680.

The Merry Milk-Maid of Islington was reprinted 12mo. 1735. *Love lost in the Dark* is from Massinger's *The Guardian.*

The Politick Whore is from Davenport's *The City Night Cap.*

Mr. Turbulent: or, *The Melanchollicks.* A Comedy. D.G. Early in 1682. 4to. 1682. Re-issued in 1685 as *The Factious Citizen; or The Melancholy Visioner,* 4to.

Love's Metamorphosis; or, *The Disguiz'd Lovers.* A Comedie. The extant MS. is inscribed "Nar. Luttrell, his Book, 1682." Although equipped with prologue, epilogue and songs, apparently unacted.

Romulus and Hersilia; Or, *The Sabine War:* A Tragedy. D.G. 10th August, 1682. *Brook's Impartial Mercury,* 17th November, 1682 advertises: "To be published on Monday next, the last new play called *Romulus.*" 4to, 1683.

The Princes Ball; or The Conquest of Queen Judith. Not Printed. A Droll, Acted at Bartholomew Fair in " *the Booth next to the Grey-hound*," August, 1682.

The Irish Evidence ; the Humours of Tiege. A Droll, not printed. Acted at Bartholomew Fair in August, 1682.

[*Mr. Doolittle.*] M.S. unprinted. *Circa* 1682–3. Almost certainly not acted. The M.S. carries no name, and therefore I have ventured to distinguish this comedy as *Mr. Doolittle*, who is one of the principal characters.

The Factious Citizen ; or The Melancholy Visioner. 4to. 1685. See *Mr. Turbulent* above.

The Rampant Alderman ; or, News from the Exchange. A Farce. 4to. 1685. (S.R. 30th August, 1684). Almost certainly not acted.

The Knave in Grain, advertised by Bentley and Magnes in 1687, is perhaps *The Knave in Graine ; or, Jack Cottington*, Stationers' Register, 18th June, 1639.

The Critics. A play acted at Norwich by amateurs, Colonel Hefford's soldiers, during the Christmas holidays, 1687. Probably to be identified with *The Rehearsal.*

Vienna Beseig'd. A Droll, not printed. Acted at Bartholomew Fair in August, 1688.

Love in, and Love out of Fashion. Not printed. Mentioned by Downes as produced at D.L. about 1689.

The Abdicated Prince : Or, The Adventures of Four Years. A Tragi-Comedy, As it was lately Acted at the Court at Alba Regalis, By several Persons of Great Quality. 4to. 1690. (T.C. May, 1690.) Unacted. " The Second Edition " of *The Abdicated Prince* is advertised at the end of *The Bloody Duke*, 4to. 1690.

The Bloody Duke ; Or, The Adventures for a Crown. A Tragi-Comedy, As it was Acted at the Court at Alba Regalis, By several Persons of Great Quality. Written by the

Author of the Abdicated Prince. 4to. 1690. (T.C. May, 1690.) Unacted.

The Royal Voyage, Or The Irish Expedition : A Tragi-comedy. Acted in the Years 1689 and 90. 4to. 1690. Unacted.

The Late Revolution : Or The Happy Change. A Tragi-Comedy, As it was Acted throughout the English Dominions In the Year 1688. Written by a Person of Quality. 4to. 1690. (T.C. May, 1690.) Unacted.

The Banish'd Duke : Or, The Tragedy Of Infortunatus. Acted at the Theatre Royal. Licensed and Entred according to Order. 4to. 1690. The announcement is a flam, and this play was certainly never publicly given.

The Royal Flight : Or, The Conquest Of Ireland. A New Farce. 4to. 1690. Unacted.

The Folly of Priest-Craft. A Comedy. Scene, St. James's, or the Savoy. 4to. 1690. Unacted. There is a variant title, The Converts.

The Siege and Surrender of Mons. A Tragi-Comedy. Exposing the Villany of the Priests, and the Intrigues of the French. Licensed, April 23, 1691. 4to. 1691. Unacted.

The Bragadocio ; or, The Bawd Turn'd Puritan : A New Comedy. By a Person of Quality. 4to. 1691. Unacted.

Wit for Money : or, Poet Stutter. A Dialogue between Smith, Johnson, and Poet Stutter. Containing Reflections on some late Plays ; and particularly, on Love for Money ; or, The Boarding-Svhool. 4to. 1691. Unacted. Not intended for the stage, being a satire on D'Urfey, who is drawn as Poet Stutter. Smith and Johnson are from The Rehearsal.

The Gordian Knot Unty'd. Comedy. D.L. Winter of 1691. Not printed. See Motteux, The Gentleman's Journal, January, 1691–92.

The Siege of Derry. A Tragi-Comedy, 4to. 1692. Unacted.
Piety and Valour ; or, Derry defended. A Tragi-comedy.
4to. 1692. Mentioned in *The British Theatre*, and probably
the same play as the foregoing with a bookseller's new
title-page. See the *Biographia Dramatica*, 1812, Vol. III,
p. 150; No. 181.

The Royal Cuckold : Or, Great Bastard. Giving an account
of the Birth and Pedigree of Lewis le Grand, The First
French King of that Name and Race. A Tragy-Comedy,
As it is Acted by his *Imperial Majesty*'s Servants, at the
Amphitheatre in *Vienna*. Translated out of the *German*
Language, by *Paul Vergerius*. Licensed and Entred accord-
ing to Order. 4to. 1693. Unacted.

The Rape of Europa by Jupiter. A Masque ; as it is Sung
at the Queen's Theatre, in Dorset-Garden. 1694. 4to.
1694.

Try before you trust. Not printed. B.M., Add. MSS.
37158, f. 17. *Circa* 1695–8.

The Indian Queen. An Opera from Dryden and Howard.
Music by Henry Purcell and Daniel Purcell. D.L. December, 1695. Not printed. B.M. AD. MS. 31449.

The Triumphs of Virtue : A Tragi-Comedy. D.L. January,
1697. 4to. 1697.

The Strollers. A comedy of which nothing is known, save
that Sir Charles Sedley wrote the Prologue, which is extant,
British Museum Eg. MS. 2623, f. 63. This has been
printed in the recent edition (1928) of Sedley's *Poetical and
Dramatic Works*, Vol. 1, p. 49.

The Fatal Discovery ; Or, Love in Ruines. A Tragedy.
Drury Lane, March 1698. 4to. 1698.

Feign'd Friendship : Or The Mad Reformer. " As it was
Acted at the Theatre in Little Lincoln's-Inn-Fields," May–
June, 1699. 4to. No date [1699].

A

ARIADNE (pseudonym).
She Ventures And He Wins. A Comedy. "Written by a Young Lady." Lincoln's Inn Fields, October, 1695. 4to. 1696.
The Unnatural Mother, The Scene in the Kingdom of Siam. "Written by a Young Lady." Lincoln's Inn Fields, autumn, 1697. 4to. 1698. Advertised in the *Post-Boy*, 16–18 Nov., 1697, as to be published during the following week.

ARROWSMITH, Rev. JOSEPH (*c.* 1647–*c.* 1708).
The Reformation. A Comedy. D.G. September, 1673. 4to. 1673. (T.C. 24 November, 1673.)

AUBREY, JOHN (1626–97).
The Countrey Revell, or the Revell of Aldford. Andrew Clark, in his edition of Aubrey's *Brief Lives*, 1898, vol. II, pp. 332–339 (Appendix II), has printed a couple of scenes from this rough draft of a comedy composed by Aubrey in 1671. (Bodley M.S. Aubrey, 21.)

B

BAILEY, ABRAHAM (of Lincoln's Inn, Gent.).
The Spightful Sister. A New Comedy. Unacted. Licensed April 10th, 1667. 4to. 1667.

BANCROFT, JOHN (?–1696).
The Tragedy of Sertorius. D.L. *c.* February, 1678–9. Licensed March 10, 1678–9. 4to. 1679. (T.C. May, 1679.)
King Edward the Third, With The Fall Of Mortimer Earl of March. An Historicall Play. D.L. November, 1690. 4to. 1691.
Henry the Second, King of England; With The Death of Rosamond. A Tragedy. D.L. September, 1692. (Publication advertised in " London Gazette," Nov. 24–28, 1692.) 4to. 1693.

Coxeter attributes *King Edward the Third* to Bancroft, who according to Gildon was also the author of *Henry the Second.* William Mountford, however, signed the dedications of both these pieces when they were published, and they are thus included in his *Works (Six Plays, Written by Mr. Mountfort)*, 2 vols., 12mo, 1720 ; but in the Preface it is said that they were " not wholly composed by him," although " he had, at least, a Share in fitting them for the Stage," and *Henry the Second* is definitely ascribed to Bancroft.

BANKS, JOHN (?–1706).
The Rival Kings : Or The Loves Of Oroondates and Statira. A Tragædy. D.L. June, 1677. (S.R. 26 July, 1677.) 4to. 1677. (T.C. 26 November, 1677.)
The Destruction Of Troy. A Tragedy. D.G. November–December, 1678. (S.R. 26 February, 1678–9.) Licensed January 29, 1678-9. 4to. 1679. (T.C. May, 1679.)
The Unhappy Favourite : Or The Earl of Essex. A Tragedy. D.L. autumn of 1681. 4to. 1682. (T.C. Nov., 1681.) 4tos, 1685 ; 1693 ; n.d. [1699] ; 1702 ; 1712 ; n.d. ; 12mo, 1728, and 12mo, 1735.

Vertue Betray'd: Or, Anna Bullen. A Tragedy. D.G.
5th April, 1682. 4to. 1682. (T.C. Nov., 1682.) 4tos,
1692; 1715; "The Fourth Edition Corrected," 12mo,
1734; 8vo, 1776.

The Island Queens : Or The Death of Mary, Queen of Scotland.
A Tragedy. Publish'd only in Defence of the Author and
the Play, against some mistaken Censures, occasion'd by its
being prohibited the Stage. [Unacted.] 4to. 1684.

The Innocent Usurper : Or, The Death of The Lady Jane Grey.
A Tragedy. Unacted, as banned by the Censor in April,
1692. Dedication (To Bentley) signed " J. Banks. Charles
Street, Octob. 5th, 1693." 4to. 1694.

Cyrus the Great : Or, The Tragedy of Love. L.I.F. second
week in December, 1695. 4to, 1696; and 12mo, 1735.

The Albion Queens : Or The Death of Mary Queen of Scotland.
D.L. 6 March, 1704. 4to [1704]; 12mo, 1728; 12mo,
1735.

BARNES, JOSHUA (1654–1712)

The Academie ; or The Cambridge Dunns. Acted by undergraduates of Emmanuel College, Cambridge, in 1675 and
1676, but not printed. There are two MSS. at Emmanuel.

Englebert. Acted at Cambridge. Not printed. This
play is in rhyme, part tragedy, part opera. MS. preserved
at Emmanuel College.

Landgartha ; or The Amazon Queen of Denmark and Norway.
An Entertainment designed for their Royal Highnesses The
Prince and Princess of Denmark. The play was finished on
29th May, 1683, almost a month before the royal nuptials.
Not printed. MS. preserved at Emmanuel College.

BARTLEY, *Sir* WILLIAM. (Possibly to be identified with
Sir William Berkeley, *ob*. 1677.)

Cornelia. Vere Street, 1st June, 1662. Of this play, which was not printed, nothing is known.

Sir William Berkeley wrote a tragi-comedy, *The Lost Lady*, folio, 1638, which was revived after the Restoration. *The Lost Lady* is reprinted in Dodsley, 1744; and in Hazlitt's *Dodsley*, Vol. XII, 1875.

BEDLOE, WILLIAM (1650–1680).

The Excommunicated Prince : Or, The False Relique. A Tragedy. As it was Acted By His Holiness's Servants. *Being the* Popish Plot *in a* Play. By Capt. *William* Bedloe. Unacted. Folio. 1679. Advertised in *Domestick Intelligence*, 31 October, 1679. Actually this play is not concerned with Oates' Plot. It has been attributed by Anthony à Wood to Thomas Walter, M.A., of Jesus College, Oxford. Making mention of *The Excommunicated Prince*, he says : " To which trag. tho' the name of Capt. Will. Bedloe is put as author, yet this Mr. Walter wrote all, or the most part of it." *Fasti Oxonienses, anno* 1680; ed. Bliss, 1815, The Second Part, p. 373.

BEHN, *Mrs.* APHRA. (APHARA *or* AYFARA), *née* AMIS (1640–1689).

The Forc'd Marriage, Or the Jealous Bridegroom. A Tragi-Comedy. L.I.F. December, 1670. 4to. 1671. (T.C. 13 Feb., 1671.) 4tos, 1678 ; 1690.

The Amorous Prince, Or, The Curious Husband. A Comedy. L.I.F. spring of 1671. 4to. 1671. (T.C. 10 July, 1671.)

The Dutch Lover. A Comedy. D.G. February 1672-3. 4to. 1673. (T.C. 24 November, 1673.)

Abdelazer, Or The Moor's Revenge. A Tragedy. D.G. autumn of 1676. 4to. 1677. (T.C. 22 Nov. 1676.) 4to. 1693.

The Town-Fopp: Or Sir Timothy Tawdrey. A Comedy. D.G. September, 1676. Licensed *September* 20th, 1676. 4to. 1677. (T.C. 12 February, 1677.) 4to. 1699.

The Debauchee : Or, the Credulous Cuckold. D.G. January, 1676-7. (S.R. 20 August, 1677.) Licensed Feb. 23, 1676-7. 4to. 1677. (T.C. 28 May, 1677.) Ascribed by Langbaine to Mrs. Behn, who almost certainly made this alteration from Brome's *A Mad Couple well Matcht.*

The Rover : Or, The Banish't Cavaliers. D.G. 24 March, 1676-7. (S.R. 7 July, 1677.) 4to. 1677. (T.C. 26 November, 1677.) 4tos, 1697 ; 1709. 12mo, 1735.

Sir Patient Fancy. A Comedy. D.G. January, 1677-8. Licensed *Jan.* 28, 1678. 4to. 1678. (T.C. 28 Feb., 1678.)

The Feign'd Curtizans, Or, A Nights Intrigue. D.G. March, 1679. Licensed *Mar.* 27, 1679. 4to. 1679. (T.C. May, 1679.)

The Young King: Or, The Mistake. D.G. Spring, 1679. 4to. 1683. (T.C. Nov. 1682.) 4to. 1698.

The Second Part of The Rover. D.G. February, 1680. 4to. 1681. (T.C. June, 1681.)

The Roundheads ; Or, The Good Old Cause. A Comedy. D.G. November, 1681. 4to. 1682. (T.C. February, 1682.) 4to. 1689.

Like Father, Like Son ; or The Mistaken Brothers. D.G. 20th March, 1682. (Not printed.) An adaptation of Randolph's *The Jealous Lovers.* Mrs. Behn's Prologue and Epilogue were reprinted from the original small-folio leaf by Mr. G. Thorn-Drury in his *A Little Ark*, 1921, pp. 43-46.

The City-Heiress : Or, Sir Timothy Treat-all. A Comedy. D.G. 15 May, 1682. 4to. 1682. (T.C. June, 1682.) 4to, 1698.

The False Count, Or, A New Way to play An Old Game.

D.G. autumn, not later than end of October, 1682.   4to.
1682.   Reissued 4to, 1697.

The Luckey Chance, Or An Alderman's Bargain.   D.L.
April, 1686.   (S.R. as " The disappointed marriage, or
ye generous mistris a comedy by Madam Beane Lycensed
April the 23rd by R.P.", 8th May, 1686.)   4to.   1687.
" This may be Printed, April 23, 1686."   (T.C. 28 Feb.
1687.)

The Emperor of the Moon.   A Farce.   D.G. April 1687.
(S.R. 24 May, 1687.)   4to.   1687.   (T.C. June, 1687.)
4to, 1688.   8vo, 1777 (with alterations).

The Widdow Ranter, Or, The History of Bacon in Virginia.
A Tragi-Comedy.   D.L. November, 1689.   4to.   1690.
(T.C. Feb., 1690.)

" The prologue and Epilogue to the History of *Bacon*
in *Virginia, Written by Mr. Dryden.*" Folio, 4 pp.   Licens'd,
Nov. 20, 1689.   J.F.   Printed for *Jacob Tonson.*"   These
were not printed with the 4to which supplies another (and
unsuitable) Prologue and Epilogue.   They are preserved
in Bodley ; Ashmole G, 15, CXLVII.

The Younger Brother : Or the Amorous Jilt.   D.L.
November - December, 1696.   4to.   1696.   (T.C. May,
1697).   A transcript of the play, made after the publication,
and of little value, is in Bodley, Rawl. Poet. 19.

Plays, 2 vols. 8vo, 1702 ;   2 vols., 8vo, 1711 ;   Plays,
2 vols., 8vo, 1716 ;   Plays " the third edition," 4 vols.,
sm. 8vo, 1724.   *The Works of Aphra Behn,* Edited by
Montague Summers.   Six volumes, 12mo, 1915.

BELON, PETER.

The Mock-Duellist, Or, The French Vallet.   A Comedy.
D.L. about Easter, 1675.   Licensed May 27, 1675.   4to.
1675.   (T.C. 24 Nov., 1675.)   This comedy is ascribed to

Belon by Langbaine, as also by a contemporary hand in the Bodleian copy.

BETTERTON, THOMAS (1635–1710).

Appius and Virginia. "Acted at the Duke's Theatre under the name of The Roman Virgin or Unjust Judge. A Tragedy by John Webster." L.I.F. 12 May, 1669. 4to, 1670. 4to, 1679. The Bodleian copy, 4to, 1679, is the Webster *Appius and Virginia,* 4to, 1659, with a new title page.

The Amorous Widow ; Or The Wanton Wife. A Comedy. L.I.F. *c.* 1670. 4to. 1706. "As it has been Acted in all the Theatres with great Applause for many Years : By Her Majesty's Servants. Never printed before." Also 8vo, 1710, in Gildon's " The Life of Mr. *Thomas Betterton.* . . . . To which is added, The Amorous Widow, or the *Wanton Wife.* A Comedy. Written by Mr. Betterton. Now first printed from the Original Copy." 4to, 1710, as " The Second Edition"; 8vo, 1725 (Dublin); Fourth Edition, 12mo, 1729; 8vo, 1737.

The Woman made a Justice. A Comedy. L.I.F. *c.* 1670. Not Printed (Downes).

The Revenge : Or, A Match in Newgate. A Comedy. D.G. September, 1680. 4to. 1680. (T.C. November, 1680). This alteration of Marston's *The Dutch Courtezan* is generally attributed to Betterton.

The Prophetess : Or, The History Of Dioclesian. " By Francis Beaumont and John Fletcher. With Alterations and Additions, After the Manner of an Opera." D.G. April–May, 1690. 4to. 1690. (Publication of play advertised in *London Gazette,* 12–16 June, 1690 ; the proposal to publish the score 2–7 July, 1690 ; completion of printing 26 Feb.–2 March, 1690–1). 12mo. 1716.

K. Henry IV. With The Humours Of Sir John Falstaff.
A Tragi-Comedy. "Revived with Alterations. *Written
Originally by Mr.* Shakespear." L.I.F. December, 1699.
4to. 1700.

*The Sequel Of Henry the Fourth : With the Humours of
Sir John Falstaffe, and Justice Shallow.* "As it is Acted by
His Majesty's Company of Comedians, At The Theatre
Royal in *Drury-Lane.* Alter'd from *Shakespear,* by the late
Mr. Betterton." 8vo. [1720]. Produced at the Haymarket,
19th November, 1707.

The Bond-Man : Or, Love and Liberty. Drury Lane,
8 June, 1719. 8vo. 1719. (An alteration from Massinger
incorrectly attributed to Betterton by the *Biographia
Dramatica.*)

BLOW, JOHN   *Mus. D.* (1648–1708).
Venus and Adonis. 'Masque for the Entertainment of
the King.' Composed between 10 December, 1680, and
August, 1687, and given privately. MSS. are preserved in
B.M., M.S. Add. 22,100 ; in Christ Church Library, Oxford ;
and in Westminster Chapter Library. First printed, 1902, by
G. E. P. Arkwright.

BOOTHBY, *Mrs.* FRANCES.
Marcelia : Or The Treacherous Friend. A Tragicomedy.
D.L. June–July, 1669. Licenc'd, October 9, 1669. 4to.
1670. (T.C. 22 November, 1669.)

BOURNE, REUBEN.
The Contented Cuckold, Or The Womans Advocate. A
Comedy. Probably not acted. "This may be Printed.
April 26th, 1692." 4to. 1692. "Printed for *Walter
Shropshire :* at the *Angel* in *Marlborough.*"

BOYER, ABEL (1667–1729).

Achilles : Or, Iphigenia in Aulis. A Tragedy. D.L. December, 1699. 4to. 1700. *Post-Boy* announces publication 23 January, 1699–1700. (Dedication signed Jan. the 10th, 1700.) Reprinted as *The Victim ; Or, Achilles and Iphigenia in Aulis.* 12mo. 1714.

BOYLE, ROGER. Earl of ORRERY. (1621–1679).

The History of Henry the Fifth. And *The Tragedy Of Mustapha, Son of Solyman the Magnificent.* Folio 1668 ; 1669 ; 1677 ; and 1690. *Mustapha.* 8vo. 1777. MS. Rawl. Poet. 27, Bodley ; MS. B.M. Add. MS. 29280 ; and MS. EL. 11641, Huntington Library

Henry the Fifth. L.I.F. 11 August, 1664. S.R. 2 Nov. 1664.

Mustapha. L.I.F. 3 April, 1665.

Two New Tragedies : The Black Prince, And Tryphon. Folio, 1669, and 1672. (T.C. 22 Nov. 1669).

The Black Prince. D.L. 19 October, 1667.

Tryphon. L.I.F. 8 December, 1668. Bodley, M.S. Malone II ; and MS. Rawl Poet. 39.

Guzman. A Comedy. L.I.F. 16 April, 1669. S.R. 27 October, 1692. Folio 1693.

Mr. Anthony. A Comedy. D.G. 1671. 4to. 1690. Licens'd 27 August, 1689.

Herod the Great. A Tragedy. Unacted ; folio, 1694.

The *Six Plays,* folio, 1694, merely consist of separate editions with varying title-pages of Orrery's dramas, which, as the advertisement of the bookseller, Francis Saunders, states : " are to be had single, or bound together."

Altemira. A Tragedy. " Written by the Right Honourable *Roger* Late Earl of Orrery ; and Revis'd by the Honourable *Charles Boyle,* Esq. ; ". L.I.F. early December,

1701. 4to. 1702. Publication advertised in *Post Man*, 20th December, 1701. This is an alteration of *The Generall*, L.I.F. 14 September, 1664. *The Generall* was printed by Halliwell Phillips in " A brief description of the ancient and modern manuscripts preserved in the Public Library, Plymouth, to which are added some fragments of early literature hitherto unpublished," 1853. Mr. Lerty, the Chairman of the Library Committee, Plymouth, writes to me that no MS. of *The Generall* was ever in the Plymouth Proprietary Library (known in 1853 as " The Public Library "). He says : " We never had any of the MSS. of these fragments." There is a MS. of *The Generall* in Worcester College Library, Oxford. The MS. used by Halliwell Phillips is not the Worcester College MS., and remains at present unlocated.

The Tragedy Of King Saul. " Written by a Deceas'd Person of Honour, And now made Publick at the Request of Severall Men of Quality who have highly Approv'd of it." 4to. 1703. The Epistle Dedicatory to the Countess of Burlington is signed Henry Playford. In the Preface the Author is said to have been a " Great Person." See a letter, 21st October, 1758, of Horace Walpole to the Rev. Henry Zouch. *The Letters of Horace Walpole*, ed. by Mrs. Paget Toynbee, Oxford ; Vol. IV, 1903, p. 209.

The Tragedy of Zoroastres. Almost certainly unacted. " Written in 1676," British Museum. Sloane MS. 1828. See *Orrery's The Tragedy of Zoroastres*, by Montague Summers ; *The Modern Language Review*, January, 1917. XII, I.

The Widow. A Comedy. Not Printed. Theatre uncertain ; 4th May, 1665. See *Savile Correspondence*, Camden Society (1858), p. 4. The " Prologue to the Widow," *London Drollery* (pp. 11, 12), 1673, was spoken before a

revival (c. 1672) of the older play by Jonson, Fletcher, and
Middleton, and is not connected with Orrery's comedy.
See Langbaine, *English Dramatick Poets*, Oxford, 1691,
p. 298.

The Dramatic Works of Roger Boyle, Earl of Orrery. To
which is Added A Comedy, Intitled *As You Find It.* By
the Honourable Charles Boyle, Esq. ; Afterwards Earl of
Orrery. Two volumes, 8vo, 1739. This collection omits
Mr. Anthony and *King Saul;* and of course *Zoroastres* and
The Widow. As You Find It was produced at L.I.F. on
28th April, 1703. 4to. 1703. (The title-page misprints
MDCIII for MDCCIII).

BROWN, THOMAS. (1663–1704).
Physick lies a Bleeding, Or The Apothecary turned Doctor.
A Comedy, Acted every Day in most Apothecaries Shops
in *London.* And more especially to be seen, by *Those who
are willing to be cheated,* the *First of* April every Year.
Absolutely necessary for all Persons that are Sick, or may
be Sick. 4to. 1697. (A farce in two acts, not designed
for the stage).

The Stage-Beaux toss'd in a Blanket : or, Hypocrisie Alamode ;
Expos'd in a True Picture of Jerry—A Pretending Scourge
to the English Stage. A Comedy. With a Prologue on
Occasional Conformity, with a full explanation of the
Poussin Doctor's book ; and an Epilogue on the Reformers.
4to. 1704. (Anon.). Unacted, and not intended for
performance. A satire on Jeremy Collier.

The Dispensary. A Farce. Not acted. In the *Collected
Works,* 12mo, 1707–8, and subsequent editions.

BRADY, NICHOLAS, D.D. (1659–1726).
The Rape : Or, The Innocent Impostors. A Tragedy.
D.L. late February, 1691–2. 4to. 1692. (T.C. June,

1692). There are two issues of this play. They are
identical save for the imprints on the title-pages.   The one
carries " Printed for R. *Bentley* at the Post-House in *Russel-
Street*, in *Covent-Garden*, 1692." The other " Printed for
F. *Saunders*, at the *Blue-Anchor* in the Lower Walk of the
New-Exchange, 1692."

BULTEEL, JOHN.
   Amorous Orontus : *Or The Love in Fashion*.   S.R. 1 July,
1665, 4to.   1665.
   The Amorous Gallant : Or Love in Fashion.   " A Comedie,
In Heroick Verse, As it was Acted."   4to.   1675.   This is
a later edition of *Amorous Orontus*.   (T.C. 19 June, 1675.
" The Amorous Gallant, or Love in Fashion.   A Comedy,
being the First Attempt, in Heroick Verse ").

C

C., W.
   The Rape Reveng'd, Or, The Spanish Revolution.   *c.* 1690.
Apparently unacted.   Not printed.   An alteration of
Rowley's *Alls Lost By Lust*.   See W. C. Hazlitt, *Play-
Collector's Manual*, London, 1892 ; p. 191.

CARLIELL, LODOWICK (1602–1675).
   Two New Playes.   Viz. 1. *The Fool would be a Favourit :
or, The Discreet Lover*.   2. *Osmond, the Great Turk : or,
The Noble Servant*.   " As they have been often acted by the
Queen's Majesty's Servants, with great Applause."   8vo.
1657.
   The Deseruing Fauourite.   " As it was lately Acted, first
before the Kings Maiestie, and since publikly at the Black-
Friers."   4to, 1629, and 8vo, 1659.
   Arviragus and Philicia.   " As it was acted at the Private

House in Black-Fryers by his Majesties Servants. The first and second Part." 12mo. 1639.

The Passionate Lovers. A Tragi-Comedy. The First and Second Parts. Twice presented before the King and Queen's Majesties at Somerset-House, and very often at the Private House in Black-Friars, with great Applause, By his late Majesties Servants. 8vo, 1655 ; and 4to, 1655. Two issues from the same setting up of type.

Heraclius Emperour Of the East. A Tragedy. "Written in French by Monsieur de Corneille. Englished by Lodowick Carlell, Esq." Unacted. 4to. 1664. Imprimatur 9 March, 1664.

The Spartan Ladies. S.R. 4 September, 1646. Also in the advertisements to Middleton's *More Dissemblers besides Women*, 8vo, 1657, and in the list of plays (1669) belonging to the Theatre Royal, but now lost.

CARLISLE, JAMES. (?–1691).

The Fortune-Hunters : Or, Two Fools well met. A Comedy. D.L. March, 1688–89. 4to. 1689. (T.C. June, 1689.) 12mo. 1714.

CARPENTER, RICHARD (1606–1670).

A New Play, Call'd The Pragmatical Jesuit New-leven'd. A Comedy. Not acted. 4to. No date, 1661 ? (The Bodleian copy has in an old hand : " I suppose printed near 1660, or 1663."). The Epilogue concludes : " Vivat Rex, Viva le Roy, *God save the King.*"

CARTWRIGHT, GEORGE.

The Heroick-Lover, Or The Infanta of Spain. " By George Cartwright, of *Fulham*, Gent." Unacted. 8vo. 1661. The Epistle Dedicatory is addressed to the King as " *Resplendid Sir*," and there are attached six poems, congratulatory verses on the Restoration, an elegy on the Duke of Gloucester, and the like.

CARY, HENRY (*fourth*) *Viscount* FALKLAND (?–1663).
The Marriage Night. " Written by the Lord Viscount Fawlkland." L.I.F. September, 1663. 4to. 1664. Licensed 16 October, 1663. In Hazlitt's edition of *Dodsley's Collection of Old Plays,* Vol. XV.

CARYL, JOHN, *Baron* CARYL *of* DUNFORD (1625–1711).
The English Princess, Or The Death Of Richard the III. A Tragedy Written in the Year 1666, and Acted at his Highness the Duke of York's Theatre. L.I.F. 3 March, 1666–7. (S.R. June, 1667.) Licensed May 22, 1667. 4to. 1667. 4to. 1674. (T.C. 24 Nov., 1673.)
Sir Salomon ; Or, The Cautious Coxcomb. A Comedy. L.I.F. 1669. (S.R. 9 Feb., 1670–1.) 4to. 1671. (T.C. 30 May, 1671.) 4to. 1691.

CAVENDISH, MARGARET. *Duchess of* NEWCASTLE (1623–1673).
Playes " Written by the *Thrice Noble, Illustrious* And Excellent Princess, The Lady Marchioness Of Newcastle." Folio. 1662.
This volume contains the following pieces, all of which are unacted:
Loves Adventures. Play. Two Parts.
The Comedy Named The Several Wits. The wise Wit, the wild Wit, the choleric Wit, the humble Wit.
Youths Glory, and Deaths Banquet. Two Parts.
The Lady Contemplation. Two Parts.
Wits Cabal. Two Parts.
The Unnatural Tragedie.
The Publick Wooing.
The Matrimonial Trouble. A Comedy.

The Second Part of the Play Called the Matrimonial Trouble.
   A Come-Tragedy.
Natures Three Daughters, Beauty, Love, and Wit.   Two
   Parts.
The Religious.
The Comical Hash.
Bell in Campo.   Two Parts.
A Comedy Of The Apocriphal Ladies.
The Female Academy.

Plays, Never before Printed.   Folio.   1668.
   This volume contains the following, all of which were
unacted :
   The Sociable Companions ; Or, The Female Wits.
   The Presence.
   The Bridals.
   The Convent of A Pleasure.
   A Piece of a Play.   (*The Blazing World.*)

CAVENDISH, WILLIAM, *Duke of* NEWCASTLE (1592–1676).
   The Country Captaine, And *the Varietie*, " Two Comedies,
Written by a Person of Honor.   Lately presented by His
Majestics Servants, at the *Black-Fryers.*"   12mo.   1649.
Each play has separate title-page.   The Country Captaine.
A Comoedye, . . . In's Grave van Haghe . . .   Anno
1649.   The Varietie.   A Comoedy . . . for Humphrey
Moseley.   1649.   A MS. (*c.* 1635 ?) of *The Country Captaine*
is preserved in the British Museum, MS. Harl. 7650.
   The Humorous Lovers.   A Comedy.   L.I.F. 30 March, 1667.
4to.   1667.
   The Heiress.   A Comedy.   D.L.   30 January, 1668–9.
Not printed.   See Pepys, 1 and 2 February, 1668–9.
   The Triumphant Widow, or the Medley of Humours.   A
Comedy.   D.G. November, 1674.   4to.   1677.

It has been noted that there is a MS., B.M., Harleian MS. 7650, without a name, of *The Country Captaine*. As *Captain Underwit*, this was printed by Bullen in his *Old English Plays*, Vol. II (First Series), 1883.

There also exists a MS., Harl. 7367, of *The Humorous Lovers*.

For *Sr Martin Mar-all* see under DRYDEN, JOHN.

CHAMBERLAYNE, *Dr*. WILLIAM (1619–1679).
Wits Led by the Nose ; Or, A Poet's Revenge. A Tragi-Comedy. D.L. September, 1677. 4to. 1678. (T.C. 26 November, 1677.)
This is an alteration of the same author's *Loves Victory*. A Tragi-Comedy. 4to. 1658. Unacted.

CIBBER, COLLEY (1671–1757).
Love's Last Shift ; Or, The Fool in Fashion. A Comedy. D.L. January, 1695–6. 4to. 1696. Dedication dated Feb. 7, 1695–6. (T.C. February, 1696.) The first edition differs in several important particulars from later issues. 4to, 1702 ; 8vo, 1725 (Dublin) ; 12mo, 1730 ; 12 mo, 1735.
Womans Wit : Or, The Lady in Fashion. A Comedy. D.L. December, 1696. 4to. 1697.
Xerxes. A Tragedy, as it is Acted at the New Theatre in Little Lincoln's-Inn-Fields. February, 1699. 4to. 1699. (T.C. June, 1699. *Xerxes*. A Tragedy, as it is Acted at the New Theatre. Written by the Author of *Love's last Shift*.)
The Tragical History Of King Richard III. D.L. December, 1699. 4to. [1700.] Epistle Dedicatory dated " Lon. Feb. 1700." At the end of Manning's *The Generous Choice*, 4to, 1700 [19 March], is advertised : " This Day is Published the last New Tragedy call'd *Richard* the Third.

Written by Mr. Cibber." (T.C. February, 1700.) Second Edition, 12mo. 1718. This omits the scene of the murder of the two Princes in the Tower, and there are other variations. 12mo, 1734; 12mo, 1754; 8vo, 1758; 8vo, 1778.

Love Makes a Man : Or, The Fop's Fortune. A Comedy. D.L. 9 December, 1700. 4to. [1701.] Dedication dated Jan. 16, 1700. 8vo, 1716; 12mo, 1722 (Dublin); 8vo, 1725 (Dublin); 12mo, 1726 (*bis*); 12mo, 1745; 12mo, 1774 (Dublin). Dicks, No. 245.

She Wou'd, and She wou'd not, Or, The Kind Impostor. A Comedy. D.L. 26th November, 1702. 4to, 1703; (T.C. February, 1703); 12mo, 1719 (3rd ed.); 8vo, 1725 (Dublin); 12mo, 1736 (4th ed.); 12mo, 1748 (5th ed.); *Sharpe's British Theatre*, 16mo, Vol. XIII, 1805; Dicks, No. 88.

The School-Boy ; Or, The Comical Rival. A Comedy. As it has been often Acted at the Theatre-Royal, in Drury-Lane with great applause. D.L. 24 October, 1702. 4to, 1707; 8vo, 1725 (Dublin); 12mo, 1730; 12mo, 1736; 8vo (*c.* 1778).

The Careless Husband. A Comedy. D.L. 7 December, 1704. 4to. 1705. (Two editions). 8vo, 1711; 12mo, 1723 (Dublin); 12mo, 1723 (6th ed.); 12mo, 1731 (7th ed.); 12mo, 1735; 12mo, 1752 (Dublin); 12mo, 1756; 12mo, 1760 (Dublin, 8th ed.); 12mo, 1771. Dicks, No. 537.

Perolla and Izadora. A Tragedy. D.L. 3 December, 1705. 4to, 1706; 12mo, 1736.

The Comical Lovers. A Comedy. Acted by Subscription At the Queen's [*sic*] Theatre In the Hay-Market; 4 February, 1706–7. 4to (n.d., 1707, anon.). 12mo (Dublin), 1720; 12mo, 1735; 12mo, 1754.

The Double Gallant : Or, The Sick Lady's Cure. A Comedy. Haymarket, 1 November, 1707. 4to, 1707 (Two Editions);

12mo, 1719 (3rd ed.) ; 12mo, 1723 (4th ed.) ; 12mo, 1725
(Dublin); 8vo. 1729; 12mo, 1740; *Sharpe's British
Theatre*, 16mo, Vol. XIV, 1805 ; Dicks, No. 777.

The Lady's Last Stake, Or, The Wife's Resentment. A
Comedy. Haymarket, 13 December, 1707. 4to, n.d.
[1708] ; 12mo, 1735 ; 8vo, 1747 ; 12mo, 1750 (Dublin),

The Rival Fools. A Comedy. D.L. 11th January, 1708–9.
4to, n.d. [1709]. 12mo, 1735 ; 12mo, 1753.

The Rival Queans, with The Humours of Alexander the Great.
A Comical Tragedy. Haymarket, 29 June, 1710. L.I.F.
as " new " 24 June, 1719. 8vo. 1729.

Hob ; Or The Country Wake. A Farce. D.L. 6 October,
1711. 12mo, 1715 ; 12mo, 1720. Doggett's comedy
The Country-Wake (1696) reduced to a farce.

Ximena : Or The Heroick Daughter. A Tragedy. D.L.
28 November, 1712. 8vo, 1719 ; 8vo, 1781 ; 12mo, 1792.
An adaptation of *Le Cid*.

Cinna's Conspiracy. A Tragedy. D.L. 19 February, 1713.
4to. 1713.

Venus and Adonis. A Masque. D.L. 12 March, 1714–15.
8vo, 1716 ; and with *Myrtillo*, 8vo, 1720 ; 12mo, 1736 (*bis*).

Myrtillo. A Masque. D.L. 5 November, 1715. 8vo,
1715 ; and with *Venus and Adonis*, 8vo, 1720 ; 12mo,
1736 (*bis*). These two masques were set to music by
Dr. Pepusch.

The Non-Juror. A Comedy. D.L. 6 December, 1717.
8vo, 1718 (five editions) ; 8vo, 1725 (Dublin) ; 12mo, 1735 ;
8vo, 1746 ; 12mo, 1759 (Dublin).

The Refusal : Or, The Ladies Philosophy. A Comedy.
D.L. 14 February, 1721. 8vo, 1721 ; 12mo, 1735 ; 8vo,
1737 (4th ed.) ; 12mo, 1753 (5th ed.) ; 12mo, 1746.

Caesar in Ægypt. A Tragedy. D.L. 9 December, 1724.
8vo, 1725 ; 12mo, 1736.

The Provok'd Husband; Or, A Journey to London. A Comedy. "Written by the *Late Sir* John Vanbrugh, *and Mr.* Cibber." D.L. 10 January, 1728. 8vo, 1728 (3 editions) : To the Reader : "Theatre Royal, Jan. 27, 1727–8." 8vo, 1729 ; 12mo, 1735 ; 12mo, 1740 ; 8vo, 1748 ; 8vo, 1753 ; 12mo, 1753 ; 12mo, 1756 (Glasgow). Dicks, No. 53.

Love in a Riddle. A Pastoral. D.L. 7 January, 1728–9. 8vo. 1729 (misprinted 1719) ; 8vo, 1729.

Damon And Phillida : A Ballad Opera Of One Act. Haymarket, 16 October, 1729. 12mo (1729) ; 8vo, 1730 (as acted at Norwich with variants) ; 12mo, 1732 (Edinburgh) ; 8vo, 1737 ; 8vo, 1765. The editions of 1729 and 1730 differ considerably.

Papal Tyranny In the Reign of King John. A Tragedy. Covent Garden, 15 February, 1745. 8vo. 1745. Dedication dated Feb. 25, 1744–5. 8vo, 1745 (Dublin).

The Temple of Dullness. With the Humours of Signor Capochio and Signora Dorinna. A Comick Opera, of Two Acts. D.L. 4to. 1745 (ascribed to Cibber). And (in banter) as *Capochio and Dorinna,* an Interlude for Music of Two Acts. Translated from an Italian Intermezzo of that Title, by the late Colley Cibber, Esq., Poet Laureat. 4to, n.d. [1746].

There are several eighteenth-century collections of Colley Cibber, none of which however contain all the plays. *Plays Written by Mr. Cibber.* In Two Volumes, 4to, 1721, has ten plays. An edition of 1760, *The Dramatic Works of Colley Cibber, Esq.,* four volumes 12mo, has seventeen plays. The best edition (in some respects), five volumes, 1777, has twenty-four plays.

The most popular comedies of Cibber, *Love makes a Man ; She wou'd, and She wou'd not ; The Careless Husband ; The*

Provok'd Husband; were included in all the standard eighteenth century Collections, such as *The New English Theatre,* 1776; *Bell's British Theatre,* 1791–2; but the texts are often those of the prompter.

CLARGES.

According to a stanza (39) in *The Session of the Poets* (*Poems on State Affairs,* 1705, p. 157) a writer of this name, of whom nothing is known, translated several plays into English.

CLARK (CLERKE), WILLIAM.

Marciano; Or, The Discovery. A Tragi-Comedy, Acted with great applause on Saturday, 27 December, 1662, before His *Majesties* high Commissioner, and others of the Nobility, at the Abbey of *Holyrud-house,* on St. *Johns* night: By a company of Gentlemen.   4to.   Edinburgh.   1663.   Erroneously ascribed by Mr. Robb Lawson in *The Story of the Scots Stage,* 1917, p. 96, to Thomas St. Serfe.

COCKAYNE, *Sir* ASTON (1608–1684).

The Obstinate Lady: "A New Comedy.   Never formerly Published.   The Scene, London."   Unacted.   4to.   1657.

Small Poems of Divers Sorts.   With *The Obstinate Lady* and *Trappolin Suppos'd A Prince,* each having a separate title-page.   8vo.   1658.

A Chain Of Golden Poems. . . . "Together with two most excellent Comedies, (*viz.*) *The Obstinate Lady* And, Trappolin Suppos'd A Prince."   8vo.   1658.   This volume also contains *A Masque Presented At Brethie, In Derbyshire, On Twelfth Night,* 1639.   *The Obstinate Lady* and *Trappolin* have separate title-pages (both 1658), the latter reading: "Trappolin creduto Principe.   Or Trappolin

Suppos'd a Prince.   An Italian Trage-Comedy.   The scene part of *Italy*." This edition is the sheets of the above reissued. To the Bodleian copy is added *The Tragedy of Ovid*, separate title-page, 1669. *The Obstinate Lady* and *Trappolin* are reissued in *Poems*, 8vo, 1662, "Whereunto is now Added The Tragedy Of Ovid Intended to be Acted shortly."

Choice Poems Of Several Sorts. "With Three New Plays : Viz. *The Obstinate Lady.* A Comedy. *Trappolin, suppos'd a Prince.* A Tragi-Comedy. *The Tragedie of Ovid.*" 8vo. 1669. This is again a reissue of the former sheets, with a new title page and the Dedication to Charles Cotton of *The Tragedy of Ovid* inserted (A 2) before "The Authors Apology to The Reader." It does not appear that any of Cockayne's plays except *Trappolin* were acted. In Duffett's *Poems*, 8vo, 1676, is a new prologue for this tragi-comedy, which was produced at the Theatre Royal, *circa* 1675.

A Duke and No Duke by Sir A. Cockain, 8vo, 1777, is Tate's adaptation of *Trappolin*, for which see under that author.

The Dramatic Works of Sir Aston Cockain. One volume. Ed. Maidment and Logan. Edinburgh, 1874.

CODRINGTON, ROBERT (1601–1665).
Ignoramus. A Comedy. . . . "Written in Latine by R. Ruggles sometimes Master of Arts in *Clare Colledge* in *Cambridge*. And translated into English by R.C. sometimes Master of Arts in *Magdalen Colledge* in *Oxford*." Unacted. 4to. 1662. A translation of George Ruggle's famous comœdia *Ignoramus*.

The best edition of *Ignoramus* is : *Ignoramus*, Comœdia ; Scriptore Georgio Ruggle, A.M. . . . Accurante Johanne Sidneio Hawkins, Arm. Londini. . . .M.DCC.LXXXVII.

CONGREVE, WILLIAM (1670–1729).

The Old Batchelour. A Comedy. D.L. January, 1692–3. 4to. 1693. " The Second Edition ", 4to, 1693. " The Third Edition," 4to, 1693, Advertised in the *London Gazette*, 27 March, 1693. " The Fourth Edition," 4to, 1693. 4to, 1694 ; 1697 ; 1707 ; 8vo, 1710 ; 8vo, 1720 ; 12mo, Dublin, 1737. 8vo, London, 1781.

The Double-Dealer. A Comedy. D.L. October, 1693. 4to. 1694. Advertised in the *London Gazette*, 4th–7th December, 1693. 4to, 1706 ; 8vo, 1711 ; 12mo, 1735 ; 12mo, 1739 ; (as revised by Kemble) 8vo, n.d. (1802) ; 8vo, 1815. Dicks, No. 199.

Included in *A Collection of English Plays*, 8vo (1711), Vol. VII ; Bell's *British Theatre*, 12mo, 1777, Vol. XIII ; *New English Theatre*, 8vo, 1777, Vol. IX ; Bell's *British Theatre*, 8vo, 1797, Vol. XXVIII ; Dibdin's *London Theatre*, 16mo, 1816, Vol. XX ; *The London Stage*, 8vo, 1824 ; *Acting Drama*, 8vo, 1834.

Love For Love. A Comedy. L.I.F. 30 April, 1695. 4to. 1695 (there are two issues). Advertised in the *London Gazette*, 9th May, 1695. 4to, 1695, " The Second Edition " ; 4to, 1697, " The Third Edition " ; 4to, 1704, " The Fourth Edition " ; 4to, 1711 ; 8vo, 1720 ; 12mo, 1733 ; 12mo, 1735 ; 12mo, 1747. Dicks No. 149.

Included in *A Collection of English Plays*, 8vo, 1720, Vol. VII ; Bell, 12mo, 1776, Vol. VIII ; *New English Theatre*, 8vo, 1776, Vol. V ; Bell, 8vo, 1797, Vol. I ; *Sharpe's British Theatre*, 16mo, Vol. X, 1804 ; Inchbald's *British Theatre*, 12mo, 1808, Vol. XIII ; Dibdin, 16mo, 1815, Vol. XVI ; R. Cumberland's *British Drama*, 12mo, 1817, Vol. V ; *London Stage*, 8vo, 1824 ; *British Drama*, 8vo, 1826, Vol. II ; J. Cumberland's *British Theatre*, 12mo, 1829, Vol. XIX ; *Acting Drama*, 8vo, 1834.

The Mourning Bride. A Tragedy. L.I.F. 28th February, 1696–7. 4to, 1697, publication advertised *London Gazette*, 11th–15th March, 1696–7 ; 4to, 1697 ; 4to, 1697, "The Second Edition " ; 4to, 1703 ; 12mo, 1735 ; 8vo, 1776 ; 8vo, 1777 ; 12mo (1820 ?), Edinburgh ; Dicks No. 99.

Included in *A Collection of English Plays*, 8vo, 1711, Vol. VIII, *New English Theatre*, 8vo, 1776, Vol. IV ; Bell, 12mo, 1776, Vol. III ; Bell, 8vo, 1797, Vol. XIX ; Inchbald, 12mo, 1808, Vol. XIII ; Dibdin, 16mo, 1815, Vol. XI ; R. Cumberland, 12mo, 1817, Vol. XII ; *British Drama*, 8vo, 1824, Vol. I ; *London Stage*, 8vo, 1824 ; *British Drama*, 8vo, 1865, Vol. III.

The Way Of The World. A Comedy. L.I.F., the First week in March, 1699–1700. 4to, 1700, two issues ; 4to, 1706, " The Second Edition Revised " ; 12mo, 1735 ; 8vo, 1777. Dicks, No. 86.

Included in *A Collection of English Plays*, 8vo, 1720, Vol. VII ; *New English Theatre*, 8vo, 1776, Vol. V ; Bell, 12mo, 1777, Vol. XI ; Bell, 8vo, 1797, Vol. XXXIII ; R. Cumberland, 12mo, 1817, Vol. III ; Dibdin, 16mo, 1818, Vol. XXIV ; *London Stage*, 8vo, 1824 ; *British Drama*, 8vo, 1872, Vol. XI.

The Judgment of Paris. A Masque. D.G. March, 1700–1 4to. 1701. 8vo, n.d. (1778 ?).

Monsieur De Pourceaugnac Or Squire Trelooby. L.I.F. 30 March, 1704. 4to, 1704. Act I by Congreve ; Vanbrugh and Walsh adapted the Second and Third Acts.

Semele. An Opera. First printed in the octavo *Works*, 1710.

The Works of Mr. William Congreve (Plays and Poems), 3 vols., 8vo, 1710 ; a second issue has general title page, 1717 ; Third Edition, revised by the author, 12mo, 1719–20 ; 3 vols, 8vo, 1725 ; Fifth Edition, 12mo, 3 vols., 1730 ;

Dramatic Works, 5 pts., 12mo, Dublin, 1731 ; 12mo, 2 vols., 1735 ; 12mo, 3 vols., 1753 ; 3 vols., 8vo, 1761, Birmingham; 12mo, 2 vols., 1773 ; 16mo, 3 vols., 1773, Dublin ; " Seventh Edition " (of the *Works*), 12mo, 2 vols., 1774 ; 2 vols., 8vo, 1788.

The Plays of *Congreve* were published with the plays of *Wycherley*, *Vanburgh*, and *Farquhar* in one volume, 8vo, 1840, with an Introduction by Leigh Hunt ; reprinted 1849 ; 1851 ; 1864.

The Four *Comedies* of Congreve and *The Mourning Bride* are included in one volume, 8vo, 1887, with an Introduction by A. C. Ewald in the Mermaid Series.

The Complete Works of William Congreve.   Edited by Montague Summers.   Four Volumes, 4to, 1923.

COOKE, EDWARD.
Love's Triumph, Or The Royal Union.   A Tragedy. Unacted.   4to.   1678.

COREY, JOHN (―― *c.* 1721).
A Cure for Jealousie.   A Comedy.   L.I.F., probably December, 1699.   Printed 4to, 1701.   (*Post Man*, 27th May, 1701.)

The Metamorphosis : Or, The Old Lover Out-witted. . . . Written Originally by the Famous Moliere.   L.I.F., September, 1704 ; 4to, 1704.

This play is founded upon *Albumazar*, 4to, 1615, by Tomkis, and the mention of Molière on the title-page is a mere catch-penny, as *The Metamorphosis* does not resemble any work of the great French dramatist.

CORYE, JOHN.
The Generous Enemies Or The Ridiculous Lovers.   A Comedy. D.L., June–July, 1671.   Licensed August 30, 1671.   4to. 1672.   (T.C., 13 May, 1672.)

COTTON, CHARLES (1630–1687).

Horace, A French Tragedy of *Monsieur Corneille. Englished By* Charles Cotton, Esq. 4to. 1671. Unacted. The Dedication, *To My Dear Sister*, Mrs. Stanhope Hutchinson, is dated 7 Nov., 1665. The Address To The Reader, which mentions that the translation " was long since writ," 8 October, 1670.

COWLEY, ABRAHAM (1618–1667).

Love's Riddle. A Pastorall Comædie ; Written, at the time of his being Kings Scholler in Westminster Schoole. 12mo. 1638. With separate title-page, MDCLXXXI in The Second Part of the *Works.* The Fourth Edition, folio, MDCLXXXI. Again with separate title-page, MDCLXXXVII, in the Sixth Edition, folio, 1689.

The Guardian. A Comedie Acted before Prince Charles his Highness, at Trinity Colledge, in Cambridge, upon the twelfth of March, 1641. 4to. 1650.

Cutter of Coleman-Street. A Comedy. The Scene, London in the year 1658. L.I.F., 16 December, 1661. 4to. 1663. Included with separate title-page (and signatures) at the end of Part I of the *Works*, The Eighth Edition, folio, MDCXCIII. Also with a half-title only in the Ninth Edition, folio, 1700.

Abraham Cowley. Essays, Plays and Sundry Verses. The text edited by A. R. Waller. One volume, Cambridge, 1906.

COX, ROBERT (? 12th December, 1655).

Actæon and Diana, 4to, N.D. [1655–6]. Second edition, remainder sheets, with *Simpleton the Smith*, " not before extant," 4to, 1656. Chetwood reprinted *Actæon and Diana*, 12mo, 1750 ; *Simpleton* was reprinted by J. O. Halliwell, 30 copies, 16mo, 1860.

The Wits, or, Sport upon Sport. The Wits. Part I, published by Henry Marsh. 8vo, 1662.

The Wits, or, Sport upon Sport. Francis Kirkman. Part I, 8vo. 1672. (T.C., November, 1671.)

The Wits, Part II, Francis Kirkman. Two separate editions, 4to and 8vo, 1673. (T.C., May, 1673.) Although traditionally upon the authority of Kirkman (1673), going under Cox's name, quite possibly only *Simpleton the Smith* and *Bumpkin* are his work.

The Wits, or, Sport upon Sport, edited by J. J. Elson, 1932.

CROWNE, JOHN (1640–1712).

Juliana Or The Princess Of Poland. A Tragicomedy. L.I.F., July, 1671. Licensed September 8, 1671. 4to. 1671. (T.C., 20 Nov. 1671.)

The History Of Charles the Eighth Of France, Or The Invasion of Naples by the French. D.G., November, 1671. 4to. 1672. (T.C., 21 Nov., 1672). 4to, 1680 (with slight variants). (T.C., June, 1680.)

Andromache. A Tragedy. D.G., August, 1674. 4to. 1675. (T.C., 15 Feb., 1675.)

Calisto: Or, The Chaste Nimph. " The Late Masque At Court As it was frequently Presented there, By several Persons of Great Quality." Given at Court early in 1675. 4to. 1675. (T.C., 24 Nov., 1675.) *The Prologue to Calistho.* (T.C., 19 June, 1675.)

The Countrey Wit. A Comedy. D.G., January, 1675–6. 4to. 1675. (T.C., 5 May, 1676.) 4to, 1693 ; 12mo, 1727, and 1735.

The Destruction Of Jerusalem By Titus Vespasian. In Two Parts. Part the First. 4to. 1677. (T.C., 28 May, 1677.)

The Destruction Of Jerusalem By Titus Vespasian. The Second Part. 4to. 1677. The two Parts of *The Destruction of Jerusalem* were given at the Theatre Royal, D.L., in January, 1676–77. 4tos, 1677 ; 1693 ; 1703.

The Ambitious Statesman, Or The Royal Favourite. D.L. March, 1679. 4to. 1679. (T.C. June, 1679). 4to, 1681. (T.C. May, 1681.)

Thyestes. A Tragedy. D.L. March, 1680. 4to. 1681. (T.C. May, 1681.)

The Misery Of Civil-War. A Tragedy. D.G., Spring, 1679–80. 4to. 1680. Head lines : *The Miseries Of Civil-War.* (T.C. May, 1680.) Reissued 4to, 1681 (the same sheets with new title-page) as : *Henry the Sixth, The Second Part. Or The Misery Of Civil War.* (T.C. Nov., 1681.)

Henry the Sixth, The First Part. With The Murder Of Humphrey Duke of Gloucester. D.G. September, 1681. 4to. 1681. (T.C. Nov. 1681.)

City Politiques. A Comedy. D.L. 20 January, 1682–3. 4to. 1683. (T.C. May, 1683) ; 4to, 1688.

Sir Courtly Nice : Or, It Cannot Be. A Comedy. D.L. 4 May, 1685. 4to. 1685. (Some copies read *Sir Courtley Nice.*) (T.C. Nov., 1685.) 4tos, 1693 ; and 1703 (two issues). 12mos, 1724, 1731, 1735, and 1765 ; 8vo, 1777. Also reprinted in *Restoration Comedies,* edited by Montague Summers, 1921.

Darius, King of Persia. A Tragedy. D.L. last week in April, 1688. 4to. 1688. (Two issues.) (T.C. July, 1688).

The English Frier : Or, The Town Sparks. A Comedy. D.L. October, 1689. 4to. 1690. (T.C. May, 1690.) Advertised as " newly published," *London Gazette,* 28 April –1 May, 1690.

Regulus. A Tragedy. D.L. first week in June, 1692. 4to. 1694. (T.C. Nov., 1693.)

The Married Beau : Or, The Curious Impertinent. D.L.

April, 1694.   Publication advertised in the *London Gazette*,
June 14–18, 1694.   4to.   1694.   (T.C. June, 1694).

Caligula.   A Tragedy.   D.L. March, 1697–8.   4to.   1698.
(T.C. May, 1698).

The Post Boy, 2–5 April, 1698, advertises publication
" This Day."

Justice Busy : Or, The Gentleman Quack.   A Comedy.
L.I.F. 1699.   Not printed.   (Downes.)

The Dramatic Works of John Crowne.   Four volumes.
Maidment and Logan, Edinburgh, 1873.   *Andromache*,
The Misery of Civil-War, Henry the Sixth, and of course, *Justice
Busy*, are not included.

D

DANCER *or* DAUNCY, JOHN.

Aminta : The Famous Pastoral.   Written in Italian by
Signor Torquato Tasso.   And Translated into English Verse
By *John Dancer.*   Unacted.   " Together with divers In-
genious Poems."   12mo.   1660.

Nicomede.   A Tragi-Comedy, Translated out of the
French of Monsieur *Corneille* by John Dancer.   As it was
Acted at the Theatre Royal in Dublin.   " Together with
an Exact Catalogue of all the English *Stage-Plays* printed,
till the present year 1671."   Licensed Dec. 16, 1670.   4to.
1671.

Agrippa King of Alba : Or, The False Tiberinus.   " As it
was several times Acted with great Applause before his
Grace the Duke of *Ormond* then Lord Lieutenant of *Ireland*,
at the Theatre Royal in *Dublin.   From the* French *of Monsieur*
Quinault."   4to.   1675.

DAVENANT, *Sir* WILLIAM, *Poet Laureate* (1606–1668).

The Tragedy of Albovine, King of the Lombards.   4to.   1629.

Possibly first acted in the Hall of Lincoln College, Oxford, 27 and 28 February, 1931.

The Cruell Brother. " A Tragedy. As it was presented, at the private House in the Black-Fryers." Licensed by Herbert, 12 January, 1626–7. 4to. 1630.

The Just Italian. " Lately presented in the priuate house in Blacke Friers." Licensed by Herbert, 2 October, 1629. 4to. 1630.

The Platonick Lovers. " A Tragæcomedy. Presented at the private House in the Blacke-Fryers." Licensed by Herbert, 16 November, 1635. 4to. 1636.

The Witts. " A Comedie, presented at the Private House in Blacke Fryers." Licensed by Herbert, 19 January, 1633–4. 4to. 1636.

The Unfortunate Lovers. " A Tragedie ; As it was lately Acted with great applause at the private House in Black-Fryers." Licensed by Herbert, 16 April, 1638. 4to. 1643. The sheets of this edition were reissued, 4to, 1649, with a new title-page.

Love And Honour. Licensed by Herbert, 20 November, 1634. 4to. 1649. Written by W. Davenant Knight. Presented by His Majesties Servants at the *Black-Fryers.*

The original name proposed for this play was *The Courage of Love* ; the second, *The Nonpareilles, or the Matchless Maids.*

The Countryman. N.P. Acted at the Inner Temple Hall, 5th November, 1657. S.R. 9 September, 1653.

The First Days Entertainment At Rutland-House, " By *Declamations* and *Musick* : After the manner of the Ancients." 12mo. 1657.

The Siege of Rhodes. " Made a Representation by the Art of Prospective in Scenes, And the Story sung in *Recitative* Musick. At the back part of Rutland-House in the upper end of Aldersgate-Street, London." 4to. 1656. Rutland House, autumn of 1656, probably in September.

The Siege of Rhodes. "At the Cock Pit in Drury Lane." Cockpit at some date before 25th July, 1658. 4to. 1659.

The Siege of Rhodes : "The First and Second Part. As they were lately Represented at His Highness the Duke of York's Theatre in *Lincoln's-Inn-Fields.* The First Part being lately Enlarg'd." L.I.F. Friday, 28th June, 1661. On Saturday, 29th June, the Second Part was given, and the two Parts were thus acted alternatively for a fortnight. 4to, 1663 ; and 4to, 1670.

The Cruelty of the Spaniards In Peru. "Exprest by Instrumentall and Vocall Musick, and by Art of Perspective in Scenes, &c. Represented daily at the *Cockpit* in *Drury-Lane,* At Three after noone punctually." Cockpit, June, 1658. 4to. 1658.

*The History of S*ʳ *Francis Drake.* "Exprest by Instrumentall and Vocall Musick, and by Art of Perspective in Scenes, &c. *The First Part.* Represented daily at the *Cockpit* in *Drury-Lane* at Three Afternoon Punctually." Cockpit, winter 1658–9. 4to. 1659.

The Rivals. A Comedy. L.I.F. spring of 1664. (S.R. 9 November, 1668.) Licensed 19 September, 1668. 4to. 1668.

The Tempest, Or the Enchanted Island. A Comedy. (With Dryden) L.I.F. 7 November, 1667. (S.R. 8 January, 1669–70.) 4to, 1670, two issues. (T.C. 17 February, 1670.) Folio, 1701 (with variants), in Dryden's *Comedies, Tragedies and Operas* ; and again (also with variants) in the collection called *English Plays,* "*by* T. Johnson, *Bookseller in the* Hague." Edited by Montague Summers in *Shakespearean Adaptations,* 1922.

The Man's the Master. A Comedy. L.I.F. 26 March, 1668. 4to, 1669 ; 8vo, 1775.

[*Macbeth :* A Tragedy. 4to. 1673. (T.C. 6th May, 1673.)] This is not Davenant's *Macbeth*, and not an alteration, but a reprint of the First Folio with the addition of three songs and a few accidental variants.

Macbeth, A Tragædy. With all the Alterations, Amendments, Additions, And New Songs. " *As it's now Acted at the Dukes Theatre.*" 4to. 1674. (T.C. 6th July, 1674.) Seen by Pepys at L.I.F. 5 November, 1664. 4tos, 1687, 1689, 1695, 1697, and 1710. This 4to, 1674, represents the " Tragedy of *Macbeth* . . . drest in all it's Finery," as recorded by Downes.

The Tragedy of Julius Cæsar : With the Death of Brutus and Cassius. " Written Originally by Shakespear, And since Alter'd by Sir William Davenant and John Dryden late Poets Laureate." 12mo. M.DCC.XIX. This stage version of *Julius Cæsar* appears in " A Collection of Plays by Eminent Hands ; in Four Volumes . . . London . . . 1719 : " 12mo. It is generally agreed that neither Davenant nor Dryden had anything to do with this alteration.

Two Excellent Plays : The Wits, A Comedie. The Platonick Lovers, A Tragi-Comedie. 8vo. 1665.

The Works of Sr William D'avenant Kt. Folio. 1673. This folio as well as *Gondibert* and other poems contains :

The First Dayes Entertainment at Rutland House.

Three Masques at Whitehall.

Coelum Brittanicum.

The Temple of Love.

The Triumphs of the Prince D'Amour. (A Middle Temple Masque.)

The Siege of Rhodes. The First and Second Part (with separate title-page).

The Play-house to be Let.
The Unfortunate Lovers.
The Wits.
Love and Honour.
The Law against Lovers.
The Man's the Master.
The Platonick Lovers.
The Tragedy of Albovine, King of the Lombards.
The Just Italian.
The Cruel Brother.
News from Plimouth.
The Distresses.
The Siege.
The Fair Favourite.

In this collected edition the following plays are printed for the first time : *The Play-house to be Let ; The Law against Lovers ; News from Plimouth ; The Distresses ; The Siege ; The Fair Favourite.*

The Play-house to be Let was produced at L.I.F. July–October, 1663. *The Law against Lovers,* L.I.F. 10 February, 1662. *News from Plimouth* was licensed by Herbert, 1 August, 1635. *The Distresses* is believed to be *The Spanish Lovers,* licensed by Herbert 30 November, 1639. *The Siege* is generally identified with *The Colonel,* licensed by Herbert 22 July, 1629. *The Fair Favourite* was licensed by Herbert 17 November, 1638.

Davenant altered Cooke's *Tu Quoque,* and his version (not printed) was produced at Lincoln's Inn Fields on 12th September, 1667 : see Pepys under that day. According to a stanza (36) in *The Session of the Poets* (*Poems on State-Affairs,* 1705, p. 157), he either wholly wrote or had a hand in a play called *The Secrets,* which has not been printed.

The Dramatic Works of Sir William Davenant. Five Volumes, 1872. Edinburgh : Maidment and Logan.

DAVENANT, CHARLES, LL.D. (1656–1714).
Circe. A Tragedy. D.G. first week in May, 1677. (S.R., *The Songs of Circe,* 11 May, 1677; *Circe,* 19 June, 1677.) Licensed June 18, 1677. 4to. 1677. (T.C. 5 July, 1677.) 4tos, 1685 and 1703.

DENHAM, *Sir* JOHN (1615–1669).
Horace. A Tragedy. Denham completed the translation of Corneille's tragedy by Katherine Phillips, under which name see for details.
The Sophy. As it was acted at the Private House in Black Friars by his Majesties Servants. Folio. 1642. *The Sophy,* with separate title-page, 1667, is included in Denham's *Poems,* 8vo, 1668 ; and again, 8vo, 1671, 1684, 1703, 1709, 1719, 1769, 1771 (Glasgow).

DENNIS, JOHN (1657–1733).
A Plot, and no Plot. A Comedy. D.L. 8 May, 1697. 4to, n.d. [1697].
Rinaldo and Armida : A Tragedy. L.I.F. February–March, 1699. 4to. 1699.
Iphigenia. A Tragedy. L.I.F. November, 1699. Advertised *London Gazette,* 1 Jan., 1699–1700. 4to. 1700.
The Comical Gallant : Or The Amours of Sir John Falstaffe. A Comedy. D.L. 1702. 4to. 1702.
Liberty Asserted. A Tragedy. L.I.F. 24 February, 1703–4. 4to. 1704.
Gibraltar : Or, The Spanish Adventure. A Comedy. D.L. 16 February (deferred from 13 Feb.), 1704–5. 4to. 1705.
The Masque of Orpheus and Euridice. D.L. January, 1707.

Printed in *The Muses Mercury*, February, 1707 (pp. 29–35). 4to.

Appius and Virginia. A Tragedy. D.L. 5 February, 1708–9. 4to. 1709.

The Invader of his Country : Or, The Fatal Resentment. A Tragedy. D.L. 11th November, 1719 (3 performances ; 12th and 13th Nov.). 8vo. 1720.

Coriolanus, The Invader of his Country : Or, The Fatal Resentment. A Tragedy. The Second Edition. 8vo. 1721. This is the above play with a new title page.

DIGBY, GEORGE, *Earl of* BRISTOL (1612–1677).

Elvira, Or, The worst not always true. A Comedy. L.I.F. 1663–4. 4to. 1667. (T.C. 26 November, 1677.) 4to. 1685. In Hazlitt's *Dodsley*, Vol. XV, and in *The Ancient British Drama*, Vol. III.

'Tis Better than it was.

Worse and Worse. These two plays, which were not printed, are recorded by Downes as having been acted at Lincoln's Inn Fields between 1662 and 1665. *Worse and Worse* was performed at Court on Monday, 26th November, 1666.

All three plays are from Calderon. *Elvira* is an adaptation of *No Siempre lo Peor es Cierto* ; *'Tis Better than it was* is from *Mejor Está que Estaba* ; *Worse and Worse* from *Peor Está que Estaba*.

DILKE, THOMAS (1663–1700).

The Lover's Luck : A Comedy. L.I.F. November, 1695. 4to. 1696. (T.C. February, 1696.)

The City Lady : or, Folly Reclaim'd. A Comedy. L.I.F. first week of January, 1696–7. 4to. 1697. (T.C. June, 1697).

The Pretenders : or, The Town Unmaskt. A Comedy. L.I.F. May, 1698. 4to. 1698.

DOGGETT, THOMAS (?–1721).
The Country-Wake : A Comedy. L.I.F. 1696. 4to [1696].
4to. 1697. As *Hob, or the Country-Wake,* 8vo, 1725 (Dublin).

DOVER, JOHN (1644–1725).
The Roman Generalls : or the Distressed Ladies. A Tragedy.
Unacted. 4to. 1667.
The Mall : Or The Modish Lovers. A Comedy. L.I.F.
(by Killigrew's company) January–February, 1674. 4to.
1674. (T.C. 26 May, 1674.)

D'OYLEY, E.
Brittanicus, or, the Man of Honour. A Comedy. Written
in ye year 1695. MS., 19 pages ; Dedicated " To my
worthy friend, Erasmus Earl of Heydon in ye County of
Norff, Esq." Not printed, and unacted. Erasmus Earle
was the son of Erasmus Earle (1590–1667), serjeant-at-law,
and M.P. for Norwich, 1647.

DRAKE, *Dr.* JAMES (1667–1707).
The Sham-Lawyer : or the Lucky Extravagant. A Comedy.
" As it was damnably Acted at the Theatre Royal in Drury
Lane." D.L. 31 May, 1697. 4to. 1697. Advertised in
Post Boy, 6 July–8 July, 1697.

DRYDEN, JOHN, *Poet Laureate* (1631–1700).
The Wild Gallant. A Comedy. " As it was Acted at
the *Theater-Royal.*" T.R., Vere Street, 5 February, 1662–3.
(S.R. 7 August, 1667.) 4to. 1669. (T.C. 19 May, 1669).
4to, 1669, a second issue, with slight variants and the
spelling *Theatre-Royal* on the title-page. 4to, 1684 ; 1686 ;
1694. 12mo, 1735 ; 8vo, 1777. The play was revived
with alterations, D.L. 1669, in which form it is printed.

The Indian-Queen. A Tragedy. Written with Sir Robert Howard. D.L. January, 1663–4. In *Four New Plays*, Folio, 1665. Imprimatur March 7, 1664–5. (S.R. 7 March, 1664–5). Folio. *Five New Plays*, 1692 ; reissued with new title-page, 1700. 12mo, 1735.

See also under HOWARD, *Sir* ROBERT.

The Rival Ladies. A Tragi-Comedy. D.L. May, 1664. (S.R. 27 June, 1664.) 4to, 1664 ; 4to, 1669 ; 1675 ; 1693. 8vo, 1777.

The Indian Emperour, Or, The Conquest Of Mexico By The Spaniards. Being the Sequel of the *Indian Queen.* D.L. April, 1665. (S.R. 26 May, 1665.) 4to, 1667. 4tos, 1668 ; 1670 ; 1681 ; 1686 ; 1692 ; 1694 ; 1696 ; 1703. M.S. (*anno* 1665), at Trinity College Library, Cambridge : (R. 3. 10.)

Secret-Love, Or The Maiden-Queen. D.L. late February, 1666–7. (S.R. 7 Aug. 1667). 4to, 1668. 4tos, 1669 ; 1679 ; 1691 ; 1698. There are three distinct varieties of the *editio princeps*, all differing in small particulars.

Sr *Martin Mar-all, Or The Feign'd Innocence :* A Comedy. L.I.F. 15 August, 1667. (S.R. as " A Comedy written by the Duke of Newe Castle," 24 June, 1668.) 4to, 1668. 4tos, 1668 (a second edition) ; 1678 ; 1691 ; 1697. 8vo, 1777.

The Tempest, Or The Enchanted Island. A Comedy. (With Davenant.) L.I.F. 7 November, 1667. (S.R. 8 January, 1669–70). 4to, 1670, two issues. (T.C. 17 February, 1670). Folio, 1701, (with variants) in Dryden's *Comedies, Tragedies, and Operas ;* and again (also with variants) in the collection called *English Plays, by* T. Johnson, *Bookseller in the Hague."* Edited by Montague Summers in *Shakespearean Adaptations,* 1922.

An Evening's Love, Or The Mock-Astrologer. Acted at

the Theatre Royal. D.L. 12 June, 1668. (S.R. 20 Nov.
1668.) 4to, 1671. (T.C. 13 Feb., 1671.) 4tos, 1671
(a second edition with *Theatre-Royal* on title-page); 1675;
1691.

Tyrannick Love, Or The Royal Martyr. A Tragedy. D.L.
last week in June, 1669. (S.R. 14 July, 1669.) 4to, 1670.
(T.C. 22 Nov., 1670.) 4tos, 1672; 1677; 1686; 1694;
1695; 1702.

The Conquest Of Granada By The Spaniards. In Two Parts.
D.L. Part I, between 10 December, 1670, and the New
Year: Part II, 9 January, 1670–1. (S.R. 25 Feb., 1670–1.)
4to, 1672. Title-page to the Second Part reads: *Almanzor
and Almahide,/Or, The/Conquest of Granada/The Second Part.*
(T.C. 7 Feb., 1672.) 4tos, 1673; 1678; 1687; 1695;
1704.

Marriage A-la-Mode. A Comedy. L.I.F. about Easter,
1672. (S.R. as " Amorous adventures or Marriage â la
mode," 18 March, 1672–3.) 4to. 1673. (T.C. 16 June,
1673.) 4tos, 1684; 1691; 1698.

The Assignation : Or, Love in a Nunnery. L.I.F. late
winter, probably November, 1672. (S.R. 18 March.
1672–3.) 4to, 1673. (T.C. 16 June, 1673.) 4tos, 1678; 1692.

Amboyna. A Tragedy. L.I.F. first week of May, 1673.
(S.R. 26 June, 1673.) 4to, 1673. The head title has:
Amboyna, Or The Cruelties of the Dutch to the English Merchants.
(T.C. 24 Nov., 1673.) 4to, 1691. 8vo, 1777.

The Mistaken Husband. A Comedie. L.I.F. before mid-
summer, 1673. 4to. 1675. (T.C. 24 Nov., 1675.) " This
Play Mr. *Dryden* was not the Author of, tho' 'twas adopted
by him, as an Orphan, which might well deserve the Charity
of a Scene which he bestowed on it." (Langbaine). One
scene at least and a certain amount of revision must be
attributed to Dryden.

Aureng-Zebe. A Tragedy. D.L. 17 November, 1675. (S.R. 29 November, 1675.) 4to, 1676. (T.C. 5 May, 1676.) 4tos, 1685; 1692; 1694; 1699; 1704. 8vo, 1777. Folio, 1701, has *Aureng-Zebe; Or The Great Mogul.*

The State of Innocence, And Fall of Man. An Opera written in Heroique Verse. Unacted. (S.R. as " The Fall of Angels," 17 April, 1674.) 4to, 1677. (T.C. 12 Feb., 1677.) 4tos, 1678; 1684; 1690; 1692; 1695. 8vo, 1777. MSS. *The Fall Of Angels And Man in Innocence,* Harvard College Library, with corrections and one whole page in Dryden's hand; Bodley (Rawl. c. 146); and British Museum (Add. MSS. 37,158).

All for Love: Or, The World well Lost. A Tragedy. D.L. 12 December, 1677. This tragedy was also known as *Anthony and Cleopatra.* (S.R. 31 Jan., 1677–8.) 4to, 1678. 4tos, 1692; 1696; 1703; 1709. 8vo, 1720. 12mo, 1728; 12mo, 1740. 8vo, 1778. Dicks, No. 96.

There is a photograph facsimile reprint of the Bridge-water copy, 4to, 1678, Printed for William Andrews Clark, jun., foolscap folio. 1929.

The Kind Keeper; Or, Mr. Limberham. A Comedy. D.G. 11th March, 1677–8. 4to, 1680. (T.C. Nov. 1679). 4tos, 1690; 1701. 8vo, 1777. The play was cut and changed when given to the press. Malone, writing in 1800, mentions that he once saw an original unaltered MS., then (*c.* 1785) in the possession of the Rev. Dr. Wilson, Senior Fellow of Trinity College, Dublin.

Œdipus. A Tragedy. The Authors, Mr. *Dryden,* and Mr. *Lee.* D.G. December, 1678. Licensed Jan. 3, 1678–9. 4to. 1679. (T.C. May, 1679.) 4tos, 1682; 1687; 1692; The Fifth Edition (1694; often erroneously said to be 1696); 1701; 1711. 8vo, 1777. 12mo, 1791.

Troilus and Cressida, Or, Truth Found too Late. A Tragedy.

D.G. early in 1679. (S.R. 14 April, 1679.) 4to. 1679.
Advertised in *London Gazette*, 10–12 March, 1678–9. (T.C.
November, 1679.) 4to, 1695.

The Spanish Fryar Or, The Double Discovery. D.G.
8 March, 1679–80. 4to. 1681. Advertised in *The True
Protestant Mercury*, 9–12 March, 1680–1. (T.C. June, 1681.)
4tos, 1686; 1690; (with four additional passages) 1695;
1704; 1717; 12mo, 1728; 12mo, 1733 (Dublin); 12mo,
1735; 12mo, 1749; 8vo, 1777. In *The New English
Theatre*, Vol. III, 1776; the text " Marked with the Variations in the Manager's Book, At the Theatre-Royal in
Covent-Garden," has been tampered with and is unreliable.

The Duke of Guise. A Tragedy. Written by Mr. Dryden
and Mr. Lee. This was to have been produced early in
July, 1682, but was prohibited by the Lord Chamberlain
(Arlington). The ban was not lifted until the late autumn,
and finally the play was given by the United Company at
Drury Lane, 30th November, 1682. 4to, 1683. 4tos,
1687, and 1699. 8vo, 1777.

Albion And Albanius. An Opera. Perform'd at the
the Queen's Theatre, in *Dorset* Garden, 6 June, 1685.
Folio, 1685. Two issues, printed from the same setting
of the type. The First Issue has neither Prologue nor
Epilogue, but in the Second Issue these have been added
upon an additional leaf. There are other trifling variants.
4to, 1691; 8vo, 1777. The musical score with a Dedication
to the King, signed Lewis Grabu, was published folio, 1687.

The London Gazette, 20–23 December, 1686, advertises
printing of score as almost finished, subscriptions " a Guinea
a Book " to be paid to Mr. Nott in the Pall-Mall, Bookseller,
" otherwise the Curious in Musick " will not have it under
30s. a Book when 'tis finished.

Don Sebastian, King of Portugal. A Tragedy. D.L.

November, 1689. (S.R. 17 December, 1689.) 4to. 1690. Advertised for publication in *London Gazette*, 9 Jan., 1690. (T.C. Feb., 1690.) 4to, 1692. 12mo, 1735 (Dublin). 12mo, 1735.

Amphitryon; Or, The Two Socia's. A Comedy. D.L. September, 1690. 4to. 1690 (two issues). " To which is added The Musick of the Songs. Compos'd by Mr. Henry Purcell." With separate title-page; " The Songs in Amphitryon With the Musick. Composed by Mr. Henry Purcell. MDCXC." In the second issue, in many copies, the date on the first title-page is altered from 1690 to 1691, with *Socia's* changed to *Sosia's*. Advertised for publication in *The London Gazette*, 30 October–3 Nov., 1690. 4tos, 1694, and 1706.

King Arthur: Or, The British Worthy. A *Dramatick* Opera. D.G. April–May, 1691. Advertised in *The London Gazette*, 4–8 June, 1691. First edition and first issue, 4to, 1691. First edition and second issue, 4to, 1691. See T. J. Wise, *A Dryden Library*, 1930, pp. 58–60. The First Issue of the First Edition has no Epilogue. In the Second Issue an Epilogue is added on the reverse of p. 51, originally blank. 4to, 1695. 8vo, 1770, " As it is performed at the Theatre-Royal in Drury-Lane."

Cleomenes, The Spartan Heroe. A Tragedy. D.L. last week in April, 1692. 4to, 1692. Advertised in *The London Gazette*, 2–5 May, 1692. 8vo, 1777.

Love Triumphant; Or, Nature will Prevail. A Tragi-Comedy. D.L. January 1693–4. Advertised in *The London Gazette*, 12–15 March, 1693–4: 4to, 1694.

Love Triumphant is mentioned in the January and February number of *The Gentleman's Journal*, 1694, as printed, but like other numbers of the Journal, this was not issued until some time after the actual date it bears.

During Dryden's lifetime the quartos of his plays, some first and some later editions, were collected and bound up with general title-pages. Mr. T. J. Wise, *A Dryden Library*, 1930, p. 57, gives reason for believing that the first of these title-pages is 1690, but no example is available. Title-pages (of several volumes) are known with dates, 1691, 1693, and 1695. "Mr. Dryden's Plays" were collected in two volumes with a general title-page, 1694.

The Comedies, Tragedies, and Operas Written by John Dryden, Esq.; now first Collected together. . . . 2 vols., folio, 1701. The *Indian-Queen* is not included. *The Dramatick Works of John Dryden*, 6 vols. 12mo, 1717; and also 1735; and 1762. The plays whch are bound up in the 1735 edition were often sold separately, although the pagination of each volume is throughout consecutive.

All For Love, *Œdipus*, *The Spanish Fryar*, *Don Sebastian*, and *Amphitryon*, owing to the fact that they kept the stage, although at intervals, appear in several of the eighteenth century collections.

All For Love is included in Bell's *British Theatre*, 12mo, 1776, vol. V; *The New English Theatre*, 8vo., 1776, vol. VIII; Bell's *British Theatre*, 8vo, 1792, vol. XVI; Inchbald's *British Theatre*, 12mo, 1808, vol. VI; Dibdin's *London Theatre* 16mo, 1818, vol. XXII; *The London Stage*, 8vo, 1824.

Œdipus is in Bell's *British Theatre*, 1777, vol. XII; and in Bell's *British Theatre*, 1791, vol. XVIII. It should be noted that the plays are often found to be bound up in a different order in different sets of Bell.

The Spanish Fryar is in *A Collection of the Best English Plays*, 8vo, 1720, vol. III; and 12mo, 1728, with separate title-page (Tonson) in vol. VII of *The English Theatre*, general title-page (Feales), 1731; in *The New English Theatre*, 1776, vol. II (as noted under this play); and in Bell, 1777 and 1791.

Don Sebastian is in Bell's *British Theatre*, 1777, vol. XIV. For *Amphitryon*, see the Introduction.

The Plays of Dryden are, of course, in Sir Walter Scott's *Works of John Dryden*, 8vo, 1808 (18 vols.) ; and second edition, 8vo, 1821.

The Conquest of Granada, both parts ; *Marriage-A-la-Mode*, and *All for Love*, are included in *Selected Dramas of John Dryden, with The Rehearsal by George Villiers, Duke of Buckingham*. Ed. by G. R. Noyes (Chicago and New York). 8vo, 1910.

Dryden, The Dramatic Works, edited by Montague Summers, six volumes, 4to, 1931–1932.

DRYDEN, JOHN, *Jun.* (1667 *or* 1668–1701).
The Husband His own Cuckold. A Comedy. L.I.F. February, 1695–6. Advertised in *The London Gazette*, 23 July, 1696. 4to, 1696.

DUFFETT, THOMAS.
The Spanish Rogue. L.I.F. May, 1673. 4to. 1674. (T.C. 9 Feb., 1674).

The Empress of Morocco. A Farce. D.L. November, 1673. 4to. 1674. (T.C. 26 May, 1674.) Edited by Montague Summers, 1935.

The Amorous Old-woman : or, 'Tis Well if it Take. A Comedy. " Written By a Person of Honour." L.I.F. April 1674. 4to. 1674. (T.C. 26 May, 1674.) Attributed to Duffett by Langbaine. Reissued with a new title-page as *The Fond Lady.* A Comedy. Acted By Their Majesties Servants. Written By a Person of Honour. 4to. 1684.

The Mock-Tempest : Or The Enchanted Castle. D.L. 19 November, 1674. 4to. 1674. Alternative title, *The New Tempest Or The Enchanted Castle.* (T.C. *The Mock Tempest, or The Inchanted Castle.* 15 Feb., 1675.) Edited

by Montague Summers in *Shakespearean Adaptations*, 1922.
Psyche Debauch'd. D.L. May, 1675. 4to. 1678. With
head-lines *The Mock Opera.*
Beauties Triumph. A Masque. "Presented by the
Scholars of Mr. Jeffery Banister, and Mr. James Hart At
their *New Boarding-School* for Young Ladies and Gentle-
women, Kept in that House which was formerly Sir *Arthur
Gorges.* At Chelsey." 4to. 1676.

D'URFEY, THOMAS (1653–1723).
The Siege of Memphis, Or The Ambitious Queen. A Tragedy.
D.L. June, 1676. 4to. 1676. (T.C. 22 Nov. 1676.)
Madam Fickle : Or The Witty False One. A Comedy.
D.G. 4 November, 1676. Licensed November 20, 1676.
4to. 1677. (T.C. 12 Feb., 1677.) 4tos, 1682 ; 1691.
The Fool Turn'd Critick. A Comedy. D.L. 18 Novem-
ber, 1676. 4to. 1678. (T.C. 22 June, 1678.)
A Fond Husband : Or, The Plotting Sisters. A Comedy.
D.G. 31 May, 1677. Licensed June 15, 1676 [7 ?]. 4to.
1677. (T.C. 26 Nov., 1677.) 4tos, 1685 ; 1711. 12mo,
1735. MS. Bodley, Rawl. Poet. 52.
Trick for Trick : Or, The Debauch'd Hypocrite, A Comedy.
D.L. April, 1678. Licensed April 30th, 1678. 4to, 1678.
(T.C. 22 June, 1678.)
Squire Oldsapp : Or, The Night-Adventurers. A Comedy.
D.G. May, 1678. Licensed June 28, 1678. (T.C. 6 Dec.,
1678.) The head-lines read : *Squire Oldsapp : Or, The
Night-Adventures.*
The Virtuous Wife ; Or, Good Luck at Last. A Comedy.
D.G. early autumn, 1679. 4to. 1680. (T.C. Nov. 1679.)
Sir Barnaby Whigg : Or, No Wit like a Womans. A Comedy.
D.L. November, 1681 (from a MS. Prologue). 4to. 1681.
(T.C. November, 1681.)

The Royalist. A Comedy. D.G. January, 1681–2. 4to. 1682. (T.C. May, 1682.)

The Injured Princess, Or The Fatal Wager. D.L. February–March, 1681–2. 4to. 1682. The headlines read : *The Unequal Match ; or the Fatal Wager.* (T.C. May and November, 1682.) The title-page has : " Acted at the Theatre Royal, By his Majesties Servants."

A Common-Wealth Of Women. A Play. D.L. 20 August, 1685. Licensed Sept. 11, 1685. 4to. 1686. (T.C. Nov., 1685.) Reprinted by Edmund Goldsmid, Edinburgh, 1886.

The Banditti, Or A Ladies Distress. A Play. D.L. February, 1685–6. Licensed 1 March, 1685-6. 4to. 1686. (T.C. 13 Dec., 1686.)

A Fool's Preferment, Or The Three Dukes of Dunstable. A Comedy. D.G. April, 1688. Licensed May 21, 1688. 4to. 1688. " Together with all the Songs and Notes to 'em, Excellently Compos'd by Mr. Henry Purcell. 1688." The headlines read : *The Fool's Preferment ; Or, The Three Dukes of Dunstable.*

Love For Money : Or, The Boarding-School. A Comedy. D.L. autumn, 1690. S.R. 4 April, 1691. 4to. 1691, (A–KI in fours), For Abel Roper. Advertised for publication in *The London Gazette*, 9 April, 1691. Second edition with new title-page, 4to, 1691, (A–H in fours), For J. Hindmarsh. 4to, 1696. 12mo, 1724.

Bussy D'Ambois, Or The Husbands Revenge. A Tragedy. " Newly Revised by Mr. D'Urfey." D.L. March, 1690–1. (S.R. 4 April, 1691.) Advertised for publication in *The London Gazette*, 27–30 April, 1691. (T.C. May, 1691.) 4to. 1691.

The Marriage-Hater Match'd. A Comedy. D.L. January 1691–2. 4to. 1692. (T.C. Feb. 1692.) 4to. 1693.

The Richmond Heiress : Or, A Woman Once in the Right.

A Comedy. Acted at the Theatre Royal. D.L. March, 1692–3. 4to. 1693, two issues. (T.C. June 1693.) 12mo, 1718, " The Second Edition."

In some copies of the first quarto, 1693, the word *Royal* on the title-page is incorrectly spelled. The pages in sheet F are mis-numbered 29–36 ; there is a cancel leaf for G3 which is sometimes found with the original. A leaf with the song, *The Country Gentlemen* (9 stanzas), paged 61, 62, is inserted between I 2 and 3. In some copies the inserted leaf I 3 has 4 stanzas of the song on recto with catchword " V. But," but the verso is blank. In other copies I 3 is not present.

The Comical History Of Don Quixote. As it was Acted at the *Queen's Theatre* In Dorset-Garden. Part I. D.G. May, 1694. 4to. 1694, two issues.

The Comical History Of Don Quixote. As it is Acted at the Queen's Theatre in *Dorset Garden.* Part the Second. D.G. June, 1694. 4to. 1694. (T.C. Nov. 1694.)

The Comical History Of Don Quixote. The Third Part. " With The Marriage Of Mary the Buxome." D.L. Nov. 1695. 4to. 1696.

The Three Parts of *The Comical History Of Don Quixote* were published together, each with its separate title-page, 4to, 1702, and again 12mo, 1729.

Part I with the Songs of Part II, advertised as published, *London Gazette,* 2–5 July, 1694.

Part II with the Songs of Parts I and II, advertised as published *London Gazette,* 19–23 July, 1694.

Part III, advertised as published, *London Gazette,* 12–16 Dec., 1695.

New Songs in the Third Part of the Comical History of Don Quixote. And Sung at the Theatre Royal, folio 1696.

The Intrigues At Versailles : Or, A Jilt in all Humours.

A Comedy. L.I.F. January 1696–7. 4to. 1697, two editions.

A New Opera, Call'd Cinthia and Endimion : Or, The Loves of the Dieties. D.L. 5 April, 1697. 4to. 1697. " The Second Edition," 4to, 1697. This Opera was originally " Designed to be Acted at Court, before the late Queen," Mary II. " A Dramatick Opera."

The Campaigners : Or, The Pleasant Adventures at Brussels. A Comedy. D.L. 1698. 4to. 1698. There is affixed an answer to Collier, " A Familiar Preface Upon A Late Reformer of the Stage. Ending with a Satyrical Fable of The Dog and the Ottor."

The Famous History Of The Rise and Fall of Massaniello. In Two Parts. D.L., Part I, April ; Part II, May, 1699. 4to. 1700. (Part II is dated 1699). The Second Part has as title : *The Famous History and Fall Of Massainello : Or, A Fisherman A Prince.*

The Bath, Or, The Western Lass. A Comedy. D.L. 1 May, 1701. (Whincop incorrectly gives 1697 as the date of production). 4to. 1701. Published 22 July, 1701, *Post Boy.*

The Old Mode & the New, Or, Country Miss with her Furbeloe. A Comedy. D.L. 11th March, 1702–3. 4to., n.d. [1703].

The Wonders in the Sun, Or, The Kingdom of the Birds. A Comick Opera. Haymarket, 5 April, 1706. 4to. 1706. The headlines read : *The Wonders of the Sun.* Whincop erroneously dates production as 1710.

The Modern Prophets : Or, New Wit for a Husband. A Comedy. D.L. 3 May, 1709. 4to, n.d. [1709].

New Opera's, With Comical Stories, And Poems on Several Occasions, Never before Printed. 8vo. 1721. This contains with separate title-pages :

The Two Queens Of Brentford : Or, Bayes no Poetaster. A Musical Farce, Or Comical Opera Being The Sequel of the Famous Rehearsal, written by the late Duke of Buckingham.

The Grecian Heroine : Or, The Fate of Tyranny. A Tragedy. Written 1718.

Ariadne : Or, The Triumph of Bacchus. An Opera.

All unacted. In the Preface the characters of Timoleon and Belizaria in *The Grecian Heroine* are said to have been designed for Betterton and Mrs. Barry. This drama must have been planned at least some fifteen years before it was actually written.

The English Stage Italianiz'd, In a New Dramatic Entertainment, Called *Dido* and *Æneas* : or *Harlequin,* A Butler, a Pimp, a Minister of State, Generalissimo, and Lord High Admiral : dead and alive again, and at last crown'd King of *Carthage,* by *Dido.* A Tragi-Comedy, after the *Italian* Manner, by way of Essay, or first Step towards the further Improvement of the *English* Stage. Written by Thomas D'Urfey, Poet Laureat *de Jure.* 1727. Price 6*d.* 8vo. 1727. A Scenario. A spurious satire.

E

ECCLESTONE, EDWARD.

Noah's Flood, Or The Destruction Of The World. An Opera. Unacted. 4to. 1679. (T.C. Nov. 1679.) 4to, 1685, as *The Cataclysm, Or General Deluge Of The World.* An Opera, adorned with various sculptures. (T.C. Feb., 1685.) 12mo, 1714, as *Noah's Flood : or the History of the General Deluge. An Opera. Being the Sequel to Mr. Dryden's Fall Of Man.* This duodecimo has a frontispiece in four compartments. The designs differ from those of the quarto, 1685.

ECHARD, LAWRENCE (1670–1730).
Plautus's Comedies, Amphitryon, Epidicus, and Rudens.
" Made English : With Critical Remarks Upon Each Play."
8vo.   1694.
Terence's Comedies : Made English.   With His Life :
And Some Remarks at the End By Several Hands.   8vo.
1694.   Translated by Echard and others.   " *Tho' our*
Translation *will never fit our Stage, yet it may be of considerable
use to some of the* Dramatick Poets."   (Preface.)

On 9th July, 1717, *The Eunuch* as Englished by Echard
and L'Estrange was produced at Drury Lane, and acted
twice.

ETHEREGE, *Sir* GEORGE (1634–5–1691).
The Comical Revenge ; Or, Love in A Tub. L.I.F. March,
1664. (S.R. 8 July, 1664.) Licensed July 8, 1664. 4to,
1664. 4tos, 1664 (a second edition); 1667; 1669; 1689;
1690; 1697. 12mo, 1715 ; 1735. 8vo, 1777.
She wou'd if she cou'd. A Comedy. L.I.F. 6 February,
1667–8. (S.R. 24 June, 1668). 4to. 1668. (T.C. Nov.
1668.) 4tos, 1671 ; 1693. 8vo, 1710. 12mo, 1735. 8vo,
1777.
The Man of Mode, Or, Sr Fopling Flutter. A Comedy.
D.G. 11th March, 1676. (S.R. 15 June, 1676.) Licensed
June 3, 1676. 4to. 1676. (T.C. 22 Nov., 1676.) 4tos,
1684 ; 1693. 8vo, 1711 ; *circa* 1712 (Johnson). 12mo,
1733 ; 1735 (Dublin); *circa* 1750–1 ; Edinburgh, 1768 ;
London, 8vo, 1777.
Collected editions : 8vo, 1704 ; 12mo, 1715 ; 12mo,
1723 ; 12mo, 1735.
The Works of Sir George Etheredge.   Plays and Poems.
Edited by A. W. Verity.   One volume.   8vo, 1888.

The Dramatic Works of Sir George Etherege. Edited by H. F. B. B. Smith. Two Volumes, 1927.

EVELYN, JOHN (1620–1706).
" Made a visit to Mr. Evelyn. . . . He read me part of a play or two of his making, very good, but not as he conceits them, I think, to be."—Pepys, *Diary*, 5th November, 1665.

F

FANE, K.B., *Sir* FRANCIS (———1689).
Love In The Dark, Or The Man of Bus'ness. A Comedy. D.L. 10 May, 1675. (S.R. 29 June, 1675.) 4to. 1675. (T.C. 10 Feb., 1676.)
The Sacrifice. A Tragedy. Unacted. Licensed May 4, 1686. 4to. 1686. (T.C. May–June, 1686). The Second Edition, 4to, 1686. (T.C. " With large Additions 28 Feb., 1687). Reissued, 4to, 1687.
A Masque. *" Made at the Request of the late Earl of Rochester, for the Tragedy of* Valentinian," In Tate's *Poems By Several Hands*, 8vo, 1685.

FANSHAWE, *Sir* RICHARD (1608–1666).
Il Pastor Fido, The faithfull Shepherd. A Pastorall. 4to. MDCXLVII. And second title-page as : *Il Pastor Fido. The faithfull Shepheard. . . . With An Addition of Divers other Poems.* Translated from Guarini. Unacted. 8vo, 1664 ; and 8vo, 1676. With alterations, 8vo, 1735.
Fiestas di Aranjuez. (S.R. 20 July, 1670.) 4to. 1670. Reissued as *Querer Por Solo Querer : To Love only for Love's Sake :* " A Dramatick Romance. Represented At Aranjuez. *Before* The King and Queen of Spain, To Celebrate the *Birth-Day* of that King, By the *Meninas* : Which are a Sett of Ladies, in the Nature of Ladies of Honour in that

Court, Children in Years, but Higher in Degree (being many of Them Daughters and Heyres to Grandees of Spain) than the ordinary *Ladies of Honour*, Attending likewise the Queen. Written in Spanish by *Don Antonio di Mendoza*, 1623. Paraphrased in English, *Anno* 1654. Together With the Festivals of *Aranwhez*." 8vo. 1671. Unacted.

FARQUHAR, GEORGE (1678–1707).
Love And A Bottle. A Comedy. D.L. December, 1698. Advertised *The Post Man*, 27–29 December, 1698. 4to. 1699.
The Constant Couple Or A Trip to the Jubilee. A Comedy. D.L. 28 November, 1699. Advertised, *The Post Man*, 9 December, 1699. 4to. 1699. 4tos, 1700 ; 1701 ; 1704. 12mo, 1735.
The Constant Couple is in all the eighteenth century (and later) Collections : *e.g. The New English Theatre*, Vol. IX, 1777 ; R. Cumberland's *British Drama*, Vol. IV, 1817 ; *The Select London Stage*, one volume, 1824 ; Dicks, No. 178.
The Stage-Coach. A Comedy. D.L. 1701. 4to, Dublin. 1704 ; 4to, London, 1705. 8vo, 1777.
Sir Harry Wildair Being the Sequel of the Trip to the Jubilee. A Comedy. D.L. April, 1701. Published 13 May, 1701, *The Post Man*. 4to, 1701 ; 12mo, 1735 ; 8vo, 1777.
The Inconstant Or The Way to Win Him. A Comedy. D.L. February–March, 1701–2. Published 13 March, 1702. 4to. 1702. 12mo, 1718.
The Inconstant is in all the eighteenth century (and later) Collections : *e.g. The New English Theatre*, Vol. IX, 1777 ; R. Cumberland's *British Drama*, Vol. II, 1817 ; John Cumberland's *British Theatre*, Vol. V, 1829 ; Dicks, No. 79.
The Twin-Rivals. D.L. 14 December, 1702. 4to. 1703. 8vo, 1777.
The Recruiting Officer. A Comedy. D.L. 8 April, 1706.

4to, n.d. [1706].   4tos, " The Second Edition Corrected,"
n.d. [1706] ; " The Third Edition Corrected," n.d. [1707] ;
8vo, 1711 ; 12mo, 1714, The Fifth Edition ; 8vo, 1723,
The Tenth Edition ; 12mo, 1728 ; 12mo, 1732 (Dublin) ;
12mo, 1733, The Eleventh Edition ; 8vo, 1760 ; 12mo,
1760 ; 8vo, 1765 (Dublin) ; 12mo, 1774 ; 8vo, 1778.

The Recruiting Officer is in all the eighteenth century (and
later) Collections.   Oxberry's *New English Drama*, 8vo,
Vol. VI, 1819 ; Dicks, No. 233.

The Beaux Stratagem.   A Comedy.   Haymarket, 8 March,
1707.   4to, n.d. [1707].   There were several undated
issues.   Second Edition, n.d. [1707].   8vo, 1711 ; 12mo,
1724 ; 8vo, 1730, Seventh Edition.   12mo, 1733, Eighth
Edition ; 8vo, 1739, Twelfth Edition ; 12mo, 1748, Ninth
Edition ; 12mo, 1749, Tenth Edition ; 12mo, 1752 ; 8vo.
1760; 12mo, 1768 ; 12mo, 1772 ; 8vo, 1778 ; 24mo, C. Cooke,
n.d. [1807] ; 12mo, Edinburgh, n.d. [1812 ?] ; 12mo, 1819.

The Beaux Stratagem is in all the eighteenth century (and
later) Collections.   Oxberry's *New English Drama*, 8vo,
Vol. VII, 1819 ; *The British Drama*, 8vo, 1824, Vol. I ;
Dicks, No. 66.

The first collected edition of *Farquhar* is 8vo, n.d. [1709].
There are editions, 8vo, n.d. [1710] ; 8vo, 1714 (3rd) ;
2 vols., 12mo, 1718 (4th) ; 2 vols., 12mo, 1720 ; 2 vols.,
12mo, 1721 (5th) ; 2 vols., 12mo, 1728 (6th) ; 2 vols., 12mo,
1735–36 (7th) ; 2 vols. 12mo, 1742 (8th) ; 8vo, 1743
(Dublin) ; 2 vols. 12mo, 1760 (9th) ; 2 vols. 12mo, 1772
(10th) ; 3 vols. 16mo, 1775 (Dublin).

Farquhar's plays were reprinted with Wycherley, Congreve, and Vanbrugh in one volume ; Introduction by
Leigh Hunt, 8vo, 1840 ; reprinted 1849 ; 1851 ; 1864.

The Dramatic Works of George Farquhar.   Edited by
Alex. Charles Ewald.   Two volumes, 8vo, 1892.

The Complete Works of George Farquhar. Edited by Charles Stonehill. Two volumes, 4to, 1930.

FILMER, *Sir* EDWARD (1640——).
Pompey the Great. A Tragedy. As it was Acted by the Servants of His Royal Highness the Duke of York. Translated out of the French by Certain Persons of Honour. L.I.F. December, 1663. Also acted at Whitehall. Sir Edward Filmer translated one act of this play from Corneille's *La Mort de Pompée.*

FILMER, *Dr.* EDWARD (1652-——).
The Unnatural Brother. A Tragedy. L.I.F. January, 1696-7. Advertised in *The Flying Post,* 2-4 February, 1697. 4to. 1697. (T.C. May, 1697.)

FLECKNOE, *The Rev. Fr.* RICHARD (?——1678 ?).
Love's Dominion. A Dramatique Piece, Full Of Excellent Moralitie ; Written as A Pattern for the Reformed Stage. Unacted. 12mo. 1654.
The Marriage of Oceanus and Brittania. An Allegorical Fiction. A Masque. 12mo. 1659.
Love's Kingdom. A Pastoral Trage-Comedy. Not as it was Acted at the Theatre near *Lincoln's Inn,* but as it was written, and since corrected By *Richard Flecknoe.* An alteration of *Love's Dominion.* L.I.F. March, 1664. Licensed, April 22, 1664. 12mo. 1664 ; reissued 8vo, 1674.
Erminia, Or The Chaste Lady ; A Trage-Comedy. Langbaine says : " This Play (tho' the Actors Names design'd by the Author, be printed over against the *Dramatis Personæ*) was never acted." This, however, is doubtful, for Langbaine tells us that *The Damoiselles A la Mode* was unacted, and such is not the case. In general his information con-

cerning Flecknoe is vague and inexact. 4to. 1661. 12mo, 1665.

The Damoiselles A La Mode. A Comedy. D.L. 14 September, 1668. Licens'd May the 15th, 1667. 12mo. 1667.

The Physician against His Will. There is a Prologue to a play of this name among Flecknoe's *Epigrams*. The piece was doubtless a translation of Molière's *Le Médecin malgré Lui*, but it was not printed, and apparently unacted.

FORDE, THOMAS (1613–15— ?).

Love's Labyrinth ; Or, The Royal Shepherdess. A Tragi-Comedie. By Tho. Forde. Philothal. Unacted. 8vo. 1660. This is contained in *A Theatre of Wits*, with general title-page, 1661. This collection has *Virtus Rediviva : Or, A Panegyrick On the late K. Charles the I. ; Apothegmes. Fænestra in Pectore, Or Familiar Letters*, and *Fragmenta Poetica : Or, Poetical Diversions.*

FOUNTAIN, JOHN (? –1666–7).

The Rewards of Vertue. A Comedie. Unacted. 4to. 1661. (Adapted by Shadwell as *The Royal Shepherdess*, which see.)

G

GILDON, CHARLES (1665–1724).

The Roman Brides Revenge. A Tragedy. D.L. December, 1696. 4to. 1697. The Dedication " To *William Gregory*, of *How-Caple*, Esq." is signed by the publisher, John Sturton, on behalf of the author.

Phaeton : or, The Fatal Divorce. A Tragedy. As it is Acted at the Theatre Royal. *In Imitation of the* Antients. " With some Reflections on a Book call'd *A Short View of the Immorality and Profaneness of the English Stage*." D.L. March, 1698. 4to. 1698. Advertised, *Post Boy*, 28–30 April, 1698.

Measure for Measure, Or Beauty The Best Advocate. Written *Originally* by Mr. *Shakespear :* And now very much *Alter'd* ; With *Additions* of several *Entertainments* of *Musick.* L.I.F. February, 1699–1700.   4to.   1700.

Love's Victim : Or, The Queen of Wales. A Tragedy. L.I.F. April, 1701.   4to   1701.   (T.C. May, 1701.)   Published 20 May, 1701 :   *Post Man.*

The Patriot, Or The Italian Conspiracy. A Tragedy. D.L. 1703.   4to.   1703.   This play was reissued the same year as *The Italian Patriot.*

A New Rehearsal, Or, Bays the Younger. 12mo.   1714. (Published anonymously).   Actually this is not a play, but a dialogue, mainly in abuse of Rowe's plays.

GODOLPHIN, SIDNEY (1645–1712).

Pompey the Great. A Tragedy.   As it was Acted by the Servants of His Royal Highness the Duke of York.   Translated out of French by Certain Persons of Honour.   L.I.F. December, 1663.   Also acted at Whitehall.   4to.   1664. Godolphin translated one act of this play from Corneille's *La Mort de Pompée.*

GOULD, ROBERT (——1708–9).

The Rival Sisters : Or, The Violence of Love. A Tragedy. D.L. September, 1695.   Publication advertised in *The London Gazette,* 7–11 Nov., 1695.   4to.   1696.

Innocence Distress'd, Or, The Royal Penitents. A Tragedy. Unacted.   8vo.   1737.   Published by subscription for the benefit of the author's surviving daughter, Hannah Gould.

GRANVILLE, GEORGE, *Lord* LANSDOWNE (1667–1735).

The She-Gallants. A Comedy.   L.I.F. December, 1695.

4to. 1696. Publication advertised in *The Post Boy*, 27–29 Feb., 1696. (T.C. Feb., 1696.) As *Once a Lover ; Always a Lover*, this play with alterations is included in the third volume of Lansdowne's *Works*, 8vo, 1736.

Heroick Love. A Tragedy. L.I.F. November–December, 1697. 4to. 1698. Published 19 February, 1697–8. (T.C. Feb., 1698.)

The Jew of Venice. A Comedy. "As it is Acted at the Theatre in *Little-Lincoln's-Inn-Fields.*" L.I.F. May, 1701. Publication advertised in *The London Gazette* and *Post Man*, 14–17 June, 1701. 4to, 1701 ; 8vo, 1713.

The British Enchanters : Or, No Magick like Love. A Tragedy. Haymarket, 21 February, 1705–6. 4to, 1706; 8vo, 1721, in *Poems On Several Occasions ;* 8vo, 1776 ; 16mo, 1780 (1779) in *The Poetical Works of the Right Hon. Geo. Granville, Lord Lansdowne.* (Bell's Edition, *The Poets of Great Britain.*)

Three Plays (omitting *The British Enchanters*), 8vo, 1713 ; *Four Plays,* 8vo, 1732 ; *Works,* 2 vols., 4to, 1732 ; The Genuine Works In Verse and Prose Of the Right Honourable *George Granville*, Lord *Lansdowne.* 3 vols, 8vo, 1736 ; including, Vol. I, *Peleus and Thetis, A Masque,* performed in Act II of *The Jew of Venice,* and *The British Enchanters.* . . . A Dramatick Poem : Vol. II, *Heroick Love ; Or, The Cruel Separation :* Vol. III, *Once a Lover ; and Always a Lover,* (*The She-Gallants,* alter'd), and *The Jew of Venice.*

GREEN, ALEXANDER.
  The Politician Cheated. A New Comedy. Unacted. 4to. 1663.

H

HARRIS JOSEPH.
The Mistakes, Or, The False Report. A Tragi-Comedy.
D.L. early December, 1690. 4to. 1691.
The City Bride : Or, The Merry Cuckold. A Comedy.
L.I.F. 1696. 4to. 1696.
Love's A Lottery, And A Woman the Prize. With A New
Masque, Call'd *Love and Riches Reconcil'd.* L.I.F. 1699.
4to. 1699.

HAYNES, JOSEPH (1648–1701).
A Fatal Mistake ; Or, The Plot Spoil'd ; A Play. 4to,
1692 ; 4to, 1696. This piece has an Epilogue but no
Prologue. It is almost certainly a burlesque. Advertised
in the *London Mercury,* 22 Feb., 1692, as *A Tragedy as it was
lately Acted, &c.*"

HIGDEN, HENRY (1659–1703).
The Wary Widdow : Or, Sir Noisy Parrat. A Comedy.
D.L. March, 1692–3. 4to. 1693.

HOLDEN, JOHN.
The German Princess. L.I.F. April, 1664. Not Printed.
(See Pepys, 15 April, 1664.)   This play, which is not to be
identified with *A Witty Combat : Or, The Female Victor,*
4to, 1663, was at the time ascribed by some to Holden,
and with less probability to Davenant.
The Ghosts. L.I.F. April, 1665. Not Printed. (See
Pepys, 17 April, 1665.)   Downes mentions " The Ghosts,
Wrote by Mr. *Holden,*" as given at L.I.F. between July,
1662, and May, 1665.

HOPKINS, CHARLES (1665–1700).
Pyrrhus, King of Epirus. A Tragedy. L.I.F. July, 1695.
4to. 1695.

Boadicea Queen of Britain. A Tragedy. L.I.F. 1697. 4to. 1697.

Friendship Improv'd; Or, The Female Warriour. A Tragedy. L.I.F. 7th November, 1699. 4to. 1700 : *Friendship Improv'd : Or, The Female Warrier,* in some copies.

HORDEN, HILDEBRAND (1668–1696).
Neglected Virtue : Or, The Unhappy Conquerour. A Play. Horden signs the Dedication, and says : " This Play was given to my Care by a Friend." D.L. December, 1695. 4to. 1696. The " Friend " is generally taken to have been Charles Hopkins.

HOWARD, *Hon.* EDWARD (1624–1697 ?).
The Usurper. A Tragedy. D.L. 2 January, 1663–4. (S.R. 4 Feb., 1663–4). Licens'd August 2, 1667. 4to. 1668.

The Change of Crownes. D.L. 15 April, 1667. (S.R. 7 August, 1667). Not Printed.

The London Gentleman. No record of production traced. (S.R. 7 August, 1667.) Not Printed.

The Womens Conquest : A Tragi-Comedy. L.I.F. early November, 1670. (S.R. 18 Nov., 1670.) 4to. 1671. (T.C. as *The Women's Conquest.* 30 May, 1671.)

The Six Days Adventure Or The New Utopia. A Comedy. L.I.F. March, 1671. 4to. 1671. (T.C. 10 July, 1671.)

The Man Of Newmarket. D.L. March, 1678. Licensed April 13, 1678. 4to. 1678. (T.C. 6 Dec., 1678.)

HOWARD, *Colonel,* HENRY.
The United Kingdoms. A Tragedy. The Cockpit, Drury Lane, October, 1660. Not printed.

HOWARD, *Hon.* JAMES.

The English Monsieur. A Comedy. D.L. Produced June–July, 1663. Seen by Pepys, 8 December, 1666. 4to. 1674.

All Mistaken, Or The Mad Couple. D.L. September, 1667. 4to, 1672 ; 4to, 1710. Seen by Pepys, 20 September, 1667. Reprinted in Hazlitt's *Dodsley,* Vol. XV.

Romeo and Juliet. A Tragi-Comedy. L.I.F. 1663–4 ? Not Printed. Recorded by Downes. Howard preserved " *Romeo* and *Juliet* alive ; so that when the Tragedy was Reviv'd again, 'twas Play's Alternately, Tragical one day, and Tragicomical another ; for several Days together."

HOWARD, *Sir* ROBERT (1626–1698).

The Blind Lady. A Comedy. Unacted. In *Poems.* . . . By the Honourable Sr Robert Howard. 8vo. 1660. (S.R. 16 April, 1660.)

Four New Plays, Viz. :

The $\left\{\begin{array}{l}\textit{Surprisal,}\\ \textit{Committee,}\end{array}\right\}$ Comedies.

The $\left\{\begin{array}{l}\textit{Indian-Queen,}\\ \textit{Vestal-Virgin,}\end{array}\right\}$ Tragedies.

Folio. 1665. Imprimatur 7 March, 1664-5. (S.R. 7 March, 1664–5). These four plays were all produced by Killigrew's company. *The Surprisal,* T.R. Vere Street, 23 April, 1662 ; *The Committee,* T.R. Vere Street, October, 1662 ; *The Indian-Queen,* written with Dryden, D.L. January, 1663–4 ; *The Vestal-Virgin,* D.L. 1664.

The Committee was reprinted 4to, 1710 ; 8vo, 1725 (Dublin) ; 12mo, 1728 ; 1733 ; 1735. 8vo, 1777. It is included in many of the eighteenth century collections, such as *The English Theatre,* 12mo, 1728, with general title-page

Vol. VII, 1731 (a good text); *The New English Theatre*, Vol. V, 1776; Bell's *British Theatre*, 1792, with general title-page, Vol. XX, 1797; but these texts when (as latterly) taken from prompt-books often prove unreliable.

The Great Favourite, Or, The Duke Of Lerma. D.L. 20 February, 1667–8. (S.R. 24 June, 1668.)   4to.   1668.

The Duke of Lerma was reprinted in *Dryden and Howard*, ed. by D. D. Arundell, (Cambridge), 1929.

The Country Gentleman. A Comedy. (With the Duke of Buckingham.) See Pepys, 4 March, 1668–9. There is an allusion to this play in a newsletter, dated 2nd March, 1669, from John Starkey, in London, to Sir Willoughby Aston at Madeley, near Stone, Staffs. B.M., MS., Add. 36,916.

The Conquest of China. Unacted. Not Printed.

See Dryden's letter, 3rd September, 1697, to his sons at Rome. *Prose Works of John Dryden*, ed. by Edmond Malone, 1800, Vol. I, Part II, pp. 55–56. See also under WILMOT.

All Sir Robert Howard's plays, with the exception of *The Blind Lady*, *The Country Gentleman* (not printed), and *The Conquest of China* (not printed), were collected folio, 1692, as *Five New Plays*; the same sheets with new title-page, " The Second Edition Corrected," 1700. There is also an edition 12mo, 1722.

J

JEVON, THOMAS (1652–1688).

The Devil of a Wife, Or, A Comical Transformation. D.G. 4 March, 1685–6. Licensed March 30, 1686. (S.R. 31 March, 1686.)   4to, 1686; 1693; 1695 (two editions); 12mo, 1714; 12mo, 1735; 8vo, 1777.

JOHNS, WILLIAM (1644–*c*. 1700).

The Traitor To Him-Self, Or Mans Heart his greatest Enemy. " A Moral Interlude In Heroic Verse. Representing,

The $\left\{\begin{array}{l}\text{Careless}\\\text{Hardned}\\\text{Returning}\\\text{Despairing}\\\text{Renewed}\end{array}\right\}$ Heart.

With Intermasks of Inte [r] pretation at the close of each several Act. As it was Acted by the Boys of a Publick School at a Breaking up, And Published as it may be useful on like occasion." Oxford. 4to. 1678.

JORDAN, THOMAS (1612 ?–1685).

The Walks of Islington and Hogsdon, with The Humours of Woodstreet-Compter. A Comedy, As it was publikely Acted 19 days together, with extraordinary Applause.   4to. 1657. Another edition as : *Tricks of Youth, or The Walks of Islington and Hogsdon, with The Humours of Wood street-Compter.* 4to. 1657. Licensed for acting by Sir Henry Herbert, 2 August, 1641.

Money is an Asse. A Comedy. Acted on tour in the country *c.* 1637. Licensed (for printing) November the 16, 1667. Roger L'Estrange. 4to. 1668.

Cupid His Coronation. A Masque, presented in 1654. Not Printed. MS. Bodleian, Rawl. B. 165.

The Cheaters Cheated. A Dramatic representation made for the Sheriffs of London. In *A Rosary of Rarities*, 12mo, [1664].

Fancy's Festivals : A Masque, As it hath been privately presented by many civil persons of quality. And now at their requests newly printed with many various and delightful new Songs, for the further Illustration of every Scene. 4to. 1657.

Love hath found his Eyes ; or Distractions. (S.R. 29 June, 1660). Not Printed. Said to have been destroyed by

Warburton's servant.   The Prologue and Epilogue (spoken by Cupid) are given in *A Rosary of Rarities*, pp. 17–19.

Jordan composed the *City Pageants* from 1671 to 1684. These were severally printed, quarto.

JOYNER, WILLIAM (1622–1706).

The Roman Empress. A Tragedy. D.L. August, 1670. (S.R. 12 Sept., 1670.) 4to. 1671. Anthony à Wood, who knew Joyner, speaks of him as William Joyner *alias* Lyde. In the Library of Worcester College, Oxford, is preserved a MS. of *The Roman Empress* which differs in many particulars from the printed text. This presents an earlier draft which Joyner had made of his tragedy. Unrecognized, and known under the name *Aurelia*, it was identified by myself in 1931.

K

KILLIGREW, THOMAS (1612–1683).

Comedies, And Tragedies. Folio, 1664. Each play has separate title-page, 1663. This volume contains :

The Princesse : Or, Love at first Sight. A Tragi-Comedy.

The Parsons Wedding, A Comedy.

The Pilgrim. A Tragedy.

The First Part of Cicilia & Clorinda, Or, Love in Arms. A Tragi-Comedy.

The Second Part Of Cicilia & Clorinda, Or, Love in Arms. A Tragi-Comedy.

Thomaso, Or, The Wanderer : A Comedy.

The Second Part Of Thomaso, Or, The Wanderer : A Comedy.

The First Part Of Bellamira her Dream : Or, The Love of Shadows. A Tragi-Comedy.

The Second Part Of Bellamira her Dream : Or, The Love of Shadows. A Tragi-Comedy.

Claricilla, A Tragi-Comedy.

The Prisoners, A Tragi-Comedy.

The last two plays had been previously printed : *The Prisoners and Claracilla*. Two Tragæ-Comedies. As they were presented at the Phoenix in Drury-Lane, by her M^ties Servants. 12mo, 1641.

The Parsons Wedding is reprinted in *Restoration Comedies*, Edited by Montague Summers, 1921.

KILLIGREW, *Sir* WILLIAM (1606–1695).
   Three Playes. 1664.   8vo, 1665.   This volume contains :

Viz. {
   Selindra.   A Tragy-Comedy.   Imprimatur Aug. 23, 1664.   Title-page 1665.
   Pandora.   A Comedy.   Imprimatur, May the 3rd, 1664.   Title-page 1664.
   Ormasdes.   A Tragy-Comedy.   Imprimatur, Aug. 23, 1664.   Title-page 1665.

Selindra, Theatre Royal, Vere Street, 3 March, 1662 ; *Pandora*, L.I.F. 1663 ; *Ormasdes*, 1664, the house is uncertain.

   Four New Playes, Viz :
      The Seege of Urbin. ⎫
      Selindra.   ⎬ Tragy-Comedies.
      Love and Friendship. ⎭
      Pandora.   A Comedy.
Folio, Oxford, 1666.

The Seege of Urbin, author's holograph MS. is preserved in Bodley, Rawl. Poet. 29.   This differs considerably from the printed play, chiefly in the matter of curtailment for acting purposes.   This piece was produced at the Theatre Royal early in 1665.   *Love and Friendship* is *Ormasdes*.

KIRKMAN, FRANCIS.
   The Presbyterian Lash. Or, Noctroff's Maid Whipt. A

Tragy-Comedy.   As it was lately Acted in the Great Roome at the *Pye Tavern* at *Algate*.   By *Noctroffe* the Priest, and severall his Parishoners at the eating of a chine of Beefe. The first Part.   (No Second Part appeared.)   Unacted. 4to.   1661.   Ascribed, no doubt correctly, to Kirkman by Luttrell.   Dedication signed K.F.   A satire on Zachary Crofton.

For *The Wits ; or, Sport upon Sport*, see under Cox, ROBERT.

L

LACY, JOHN (?——1681).

The Old Troop : Or, Monsieur Raggou.   4to.   1672.   Seen by Pepys at D.L., 31st July, 1668, as " now new acted."

Sauny the Scott : Or, The Taming of the Shrew.   A Comedy. D.L. 9 April, 1667.   4to.   1698.   " As it is now Acted at the Theatre Royal."   " And Never before Printed." (Advertised *Post Boy*, 20–23 Nov., 1697.)   4to, 1708 as *Sauny the Scot ; Or, The Taming of the Shrew* ; 12mo, 1714.

The Dumb Lady : Or, The Farriar Made Physician.   D.L. 1669.   4to.   1672.

Sr Hercules Buffoon : Or The Poetical Squire.   A Comedy. D.G. April–May, 1682.   4to.   1684.

The Dramatic Works of John Lacy, Comedian.   Edinburgh, 1875.   Maidment and Logan.

LEANERD, JOHN.

The Country Innocence : Or, The Chamber-Maid Turn'd Quaker.   A Comedy.   With Alterations and Amendments. (Adapted from Thomas Brewer's *The Countrie Girl.*   A Comedy.   4to, 1647.)   D.L.   March 1676–7.   Licensed Apr. 6, 1677.   4to, 1677.   Also with title-page : " *A Comedy Call'd The Country, Innocence : Or, The Chamber-Maid Turn'd Quaker,*" 4to, 1677.

The Rambling Justice, Or The Jealous Husbands. With the Humours of Sir John Twiford. D.L. February, 1677–8. Licensed March 13, 1678. 4to. 1678 ; 4to, 1694.

The Counterfeits, A Comedy. D.G. May, 1678. Licensed Aug. 29, 1678. 4to, 1679.

LEE, NATHANIEL (1649–1692).

The Tragedy Of Nero, Emperour of Rome : D.L. 16th May, 1674. 4to. 1675. (T.C. June, 1675.) 4tos, 1692 ; 1696.

Sophonisba, Or Hannibal's Overthrow. A Tragedy. D.L. 30th April, 1675. 4to, 1676. (T.C. November, 1675.) 4tos, 1681 ; 1685 ; 1691 ; 1693 ; 1697 ; 1704 ; 1709 ; 1712. 8vo, 1725 (Dublin). 12mo, 1726 ; 12mo, 1735.

Gloriana, Or The Court of Augustus Caesar. D.L. 29th January, 1675–6. (T.C. May, 1676.) 4to, 1676 ; 4to, 1699. 8vo, 1777.

The Rival Queens, Or, The Death Of Alexander The Great. D.L. January, 1676–7. 4to. 1677. (T.C. November, 1677.) 4tos, 1684 ; 1690 ; 1694, called " The Second Edition " ; 1699 ; 1702, called " The Fourth Edition " ; 1704, called " The Fifth Edition " ; 12mo, 1725 ; 12mo, 1735 ; 8vo, 1776 ; 12mo, 1793 ; in Sharpe's *British Theatre,* Vol. XV, 1805 ; Dicks, No. 83.

Alexander The Great, as altered from *The Rival Queens,* 8vo. 1770.

In the Advertisement prefixed to *The Rival Queens ; Or, Alexander the Great,* A Tragedy, Written by Nathaniel Lee, Gent. With Alterations, As it is now performed at the Theatres-Royal In Drury-Lane and Covent Garden, London : Printed for T. Lowndes ; T. Tongman ; C. Corbet ; T. Caslon ; W. Nicoll ; S. Bladon ; and M. Waller, 8vo, 1776, it is remarked : " There is perhaps no Play in the *English* drama, which has received so many alterations as Mr. Lee's

Tragedy of *The Rival Queens, or Alexander the Great.* . . . The original Play may at any time be purchased at a small price, which is not the case with the modern one. We have therefore chosen to give the whole as it is now represented at the Theatres."

In Bell's *British Theatre,* Vol. XVIII, 8vo, 1778, is given *Alexander the Great,* A Tragedy, Written by Nathaniel Lee, *Gent.* With Alterations As Performed at the Theatre-Royal in Drury Lane. Regulated from the Prompt-Book, By Permission *of the* Managers, By Mr. Hopkins, Prompter. A note observes : " *The alterations and additions in this Play, on comparing it with the original, were found so numerous, and so judiciously connected with the words of the Author, that it was judged impracticable to restore the necessary omissions, without greatly embarrassing the Reader. The Editor has therefore thought it advisable to deviate from his general plan, and give the Play to the Public as literally delivered in the representation ; with the original Dedication, Prologue and Epilogue, and a Poem, addressed to the Author by Mr. Dryden.*"

As *Alexander the Great,* Lee's *The Rival Queens,* was being acted as late as 1840, but it will be readily understood how untrustworthy are the texts, printed for the most part from the Prompt-book of an adaptation of the original tragedy.

Mithridates King of Pontus : A Tragedy. D.L. January, 1677–8. 4to. 1678. (T.C. June, 1678.) 4tos, 1685 ; 1693 ; 1697 ; 1702 ; 1711. 12mo, 1728.

Cæsar Borgia ; Son Of Pope Alexander The Sixth. A Tragedy. D.G. September, 1679. 4to. 1680. (T.C. November, 1679.) 4tos, 1696 ; 1711.

Œdipus : A Tragedy. The Authors, Mr. *Dryden* and Mr. *Lee.* D.G. December, 1678. Licensed Jan. 3, 1678-9. 4to. 1679. (T.C. May, 1679.) 4tos, 1682 ; 1687 ; 1692 ;

The Fifth Edition, n.d. [1694; often erroneously said to be 1696]; 1701; 1711. 8vo, 1777. 12mo, 1791.

Theodosius : Or, The Force of Love. A Tragedy. D.G. autumn of 1680. 4to. 1680. (T.C. November, 1680.) 4tos, 1684; 1692; 1697; 1708. 12mo, 1727; 12mo, 1734; 12mo, 1761. 8vo, 1777. 12mo, 1793.

Lucius Junius Brutus ; Father of his Country. A Tragedy. D.G. December, 1680. Prohibited by an Order of the Lord Chamberlaine, 11th December, 1680. 4to. 1681. (T.C. June, 1681, as " acted at the Duke's Theatre for six days ; but then prohibited."). 4to, 1708. 12mo, 1791.

The Princess of Cleve. D.G. 1681. 4to. 1689. (T.C. May, 1689.) 4to, 1697.

The Duke of Guise. A Tragedy. Written by Mr. Dryden, and Mr. Lee. This was to have been produced early in July, 1682, but was prohibited by the Lord Chamberlain (Arlington). The ban was not lifted until the late autumn, and finally the play was given by the United Companies at Drury Lane, 30th November, 1682. 4tos, 1683 ; 1687, and 1699.

Constantine The Great. A Tragedy. D.L. 12th November, 1683. 4to, 1684.

The Massacre Of Paris. A Tragedy. D.L. October, 1689. 4to. 1690. (T.C. *The Massacre at Paris*, November, 1689.)

The first, or in some cases the second or third, quartos of Lee were collected and bound up with a general title-page, which in one sense constitutes the first collected edition. There are extant title-pages dated 1691, 1694 and 1697.

The Works of Mr. Nathaniel Lee, 2 vols., 8vo, 1713 ; *The Works of Mr. Nathaniel Lee*, 3 vols., sm. 8vo, 1722 ; *The Dramatick Works of Mr. Nathaniel Lee*, 3 vols., sm. 8vo, 1734. Each play has separate title-page, but *Œdipus* is 1733.

The pagination of each play is distinct.   Some copies have a frontispiece to Volume I, a portrait of Dryden.

LESLEY, Rev. GEORGE (——1701).
  Dives Doom ; or The Rich Man's Misery. 8vo.   1675.
  Fire and Brimstone ; or The Destruction of Sodom. 8vo. 1675, and 1684.
  Abraham's Faith. A Divine Dialogue.   8vo.   1675, and 1684.
  These three pieces were not designed for the theatre.

LISTER, MARTIN (1638 ?–1712).
  Eunuchus. Translated from Terence.   Unacted.   Not Printed.   Bodley, MS. Lister 23.

LOWER, *Sir* WILLIAM (1600 ?–1662).
  The Phaenix in her flames. A Tragedy.   The Scene, Arabia.   The Author, Master William Lower.   Unacted. 4to.   1639.
  Polyeuctes, Or The Martyr. A Tragedy.   By Sr William Lower.   Unacted.   4to.   1655.
  Horatius : A Roman Tragedie.   Unacted.   4to.   1656.
  The Three Dorothies ; Or Jodelet Box'd.   A Comedy. Translated from Scarron in 1657 by Sir William Lower, Knt.   Unacted.   Not Printed.   The original MS. was formerly in the Skeffington collection.
  The Enchanted Lovers : A Pastoral.   Unacted.   12mo. Hage : Adrian Vlack.   1658 (June).   Reissued with a new title-page *for Fr. Kirkman.*   12mo.   1661.
  The Noble Ingratitude. A Pastoral Tragi-Comedy.   Unacted. Hage, *John Ramzey.*   12mo.   1659.
  The Amorous Fantasme. A Tragi-Comedy.   Acted at Court.   Hage, *John Ramzey.*   12mo.   1660.
  The Enchanted Lovers ; The Noble Ingratitude ; The Amorous

Fantasme were collected in one volume, 12mo, 1661, as *Three New Playes*. *The Enchanted Lovers* which is placed second retains the Hague title-page ; the first and third are furnished each with a new title-page bearing the same imprint as the general title-page.

Don Japhet of Armenia. Unacted. 1657. Translated from Scarron. Not Printed. The author's MS. is preserved in the British Museum. Add. MS. 28723.

M

M., W.
The Huntingdon Divertisement, " Or, An Enterlude For the Generall Entertainment at the County-Feast, Held at Merchant-Taylors Hall, June 20, 1678." Licensed *May* 16, 1678. Roger L'Estrange. 4to. 1678.

M., W.
The Female Wits ; or, The Triumvirate Of Poets at Rehearsal. A Comedy. D.L. 1697. 4to. 1704. The *Biographia Dramatica* gives a 4to, 1697. A satire on Mrs. Manley, Mrs. Trotter, and Mrs. Pix.

MAIDWELL, LEWIS (*c.* 1648–1720).
The Loving Enemies. A Comedy. D.G. early in 1680. (T.C. May, 1680.) Advertised in *The True News : or Mercurius Anglicus*, 12–15 May, 1680. In *Mercurius Civicus : or, The City Mercury*, 12 May, 1680. 4to. 1680.

MANLEY, *Mrs.* MARY DE LA RIVIERE (1672–1724).
The Lost Lover ; Or, The Jealous Husband. A Comedy. D.L. January, 1695–6. 4to. 1696. (T.C. June, 1696.)
The Royal Mischief. A Tragedy. L.I.F. March 1695–6. 4to. 1696. (T.C. June, 1696.)

Almyna : Or, The Arabian Vow. A Tragedy. Haymarket, 16 December, 1706. 4to. 1707; 4to, 1717.

Lucius, The First Christian King of Britain. A Tragedy. D.L. 11 May, 1717. 4to, 1717; 4to, 1720.

The Court Legacy. A New Ballad Opera. 8vo. 1733. (By the Author of the *New Atlantis* ?)

MANNING, FRANCIS.

The Generous Choice. A Comedy. L.I.F. February, 1699–1700. 4to. 1700. Published *Post Boy,* 19 March, 1699–1700.

All For The Better ; Or, The Infallible Cure. A Comedy. D.L. 1703. 4to. 1703. (Anon.)

MEDBOURNE, MATTHEW (?—1679).

St Cecily : Or, The Converted Twins. A Christian Tragedy. Written by E.M. *Never before Published.* Licensed June 11, 1666. 4to. 1666. *London,* Printed by *J. Streater.* Also reissued with new title-page as *The Converted Twins.* A Tragedy. Written by *E. M. Never before Published. London,* Printed for *Robert Pawlett,* at the Bible in *Chancery lane,* 1667.

This play was probably unacted. The Dedication to the Queen-Consort is signed M. Medburne, who was certainly the author. This is also implied in the verses *Exomologesis Apologetica,* signed *M. M.,* which are prefixed.

Tartuffe : Or, The French Puritan. A Comedy. Written in French by *Moliere,* and Render'd into English, with much Addition and Advantage, by *M. Medbourne,* Servant to His Royal Highness. (S.R. 28 June, 1670.) D.L. about March, 1670. 4to. 1670. (T.C. June, 1670.) 4to, 1707.

MILTON, JOHN (1608–1674).

Arcades. " Part of an Entertainment presented to the Countess Dowager of *Darby* at Harefield." In *Poems,* 1633.

A Maske Presented At Ludlow Castle, 1634 : On Michaelmasse Night. 4to. 1637. The stage history of *Comus* belongs to the eighteenth and nineteenth centuries. With some alteration by Dr. Dalton, it was given at Drury Lane, 4 March, 1738, with Quin as Comus ; Mrs. Cibber, the Lady ; and Mrs. Clive, Euphrosyne. 8vo. 1738. With variants it held the stage until 1843.

Comus was also altered by George Colman, and printed 8vo, 1772 ; 8vo, 1780.

In Sharpe's *British Theatre*, Vol. XVIII, 1805, is included *Comus*. " A Masque. Altered from John Milton." In R. Cumberland's *The British Drama*, Vol. II, 1817, we have : *Masque of Comus*. By John Milton. Adapted for Theatrical Representation, *As first performed at the* Theatre-Royal, Covent Garden, in the year 1744.

Samson Agonistes, A Dramatic Poem. " This work never was intended " to the Stage. 8vo. 1671. (T.C. 22 Nov. 1670.)

MOTTEUX, PETER ANTHONY (1663–1718).
Love's a Jest. A Comedy. L.I.F. June, 1696. 4to. 1696.
The Loves of Mars and Venus. A Play Set to Music. L.I.F. 14 November, 1696. 4to. 1697. (See Ravenscroft, *The Anatomist*.)
The Novelty. Every Act a Play. Being A Short Pastoral, Comedy, Masque, Tragedy, and Farce after the *Italian* Manner. L.I.F. 8 June, 1697. 4to. 1697.
Europe's Revels for the Peace and His Majestie's Happy Return. A Musical Interlude. L.I.F. November, 1697. 4to. 1697. Music by Eccles.
Beauty in Distress. A Tragedy. L.I.F. April, 1698. Advertised, *Protestant Mercury*, 24–29 June, 1698. 4to.

1698. " With a Discourse of the Lawfulness & Unlawful-
ness of Plays."

The Island Princess, Or The Generous Portugese. Made into
an Opera. Drury Lane, January, 1699. 4to, 1699;
12mo, 1724. A MS. full score and libretto may be found
in the B.M. Add. MS. 15318.

*The Four Seasons, or Love in Every Age. A Musical
Interlude.* D.L. January, 1699. 4to. 1699. Printed at
the end of *The Island Princess.* Set by Jeremiah Clarke.

Acis and Galatea. D.L. 1701. 4to, no date [1701].
8vo. 1723.

Britain's Happiness. A Musical Interlude. Perform'd
at both the Theatres. Being part of the Entertainment
Subscrib'd for by the Nobility. 4to. 1704.

Arsinoe, Queen of Cyprus. An Opera, After the *Italian*
Manner. D.L. Tuesday, 16 January, 1705. 4to, 1705;
4to, 1707. Translated by Motteux from Tomaso Stanzani.
Music by Thomas Clayton.

Farewell Folly : or, The Younger the Wiser. A Comedy.
. . . With a Musical Interlude, call'd *The Mountebank : or,
The Humours of the Fair.* D.L. 18 January, 1705. 4to
1707.

The Amorous Miser : Or, The Younger the Wiser. A
Comedy. 4to. 1705.

The Temple of Love : A Pastoral Opera. English'd from
the *Italian.* All sung to the same Musick. By Signior
J. Saggione, Haymarket, Thursday, 7 March, 1706. 4to.
1706.

Thomyris, Queen of Scythia. An Opera as it is Perform'd
at the Theatre Royal in Drury-Lane, Tuesday, 1 April, 1707.
4to, 1707 ; As *The Royal Amazon,* 4to, 1708. This is the
First Edition of *Thomyris* with a cancel title. 8vo, 1709.
(This opera is partly English and partly Italian.) The

Music by Scarlatti and Buononcini was adapted by Pepsuch, with additions from Agostino Steffani.

Love's Triumph. An Opera. Haymarket, Thursday, 26 February, 1708. 4to. 1708. Adapted from Cardinal Ottoboni's *La Pastorella.* The music by Cesarini Giovannini del Violone and Francesco Gasparini.

Love Dragoon'd. A Farce. Apparently not printed. Giles Jacob, *Poetical Register,* 1719, p. 334. This is merely *The Amorous Miser,* which was perhaps acted under this name.

MOUNTFORD (MOUNTFORT), WILLIAM (1664–1692).

The Life and Death Of Doctor Faustus, Made into a Farce. By Mr. Mountford. "With the Humours of *Harlequin* and *Scaramouche :* As they were several times Acted by Mr. *Lee* and Mr. *Jevon* At the Queens Theatre in *Dorset* Garden. Newly Revived, at the Theatre in *Lincoln's Inn Fields,* With *Songs* and *Dances* between the *Acts.*" Probably first acted in December, 1685, or during January, 1686. 4to. 1697.

The Injur'd Lovers : Or, The Ambitious Father. A Tragedy. D.L. 6 February, 1687–8. Licensed March 8, 1687-8. 4to. 1688. (Sometimes with an errata leaf.)

The Successfull Straingers. A Trage- Comedy. D.L. December, 1689. Licensed 27 January, 1689–90. 4to, 1690 ; 4to, 1696. This 4to 1696 is the first edition with cancel title (*dated* 1696), *The Successful Strangers.*

Greenwich-Park : A Comedy. D.L. April, 1691. Advertised *London Gazette,* 21–25 May, 1691. 4to, 1691; 8vo, 1777.

Zelmane : Or, The Corinthian Queen. A Tragedy. L.I.F. December, 1704. 4to. 1705. (T.C. Feb. 1705.) "The following Poem was a piece left unfinished by Mr. *M——t,* who in his life was generally belov'd and encourag'd in what he did by all." *The Epistle Dedicatory.*

Six Plays Written by Mr. Mountfort. Two Volumes. 12mo. 1720.

N

N. N.

Romes Follies : or, The Amorous Fryars. As it was lately Acted at a Person of Qualitie's House. 4to. 1681. Printed for *N. Nowell.*

A MS. note in one copy of this quarto gives 27 January, 1681–2, and it is probable that the play was privately presented at Thanet House, Aldersgate, on this day.

NEVILLE, ROBERT.

The Poor Scholar. A Comedy. " Written by Robert Nevile, Fellow of Kings Colledge in Cambridge." 4to. 1662. Probably unacted.

NORTON, RICHARD (?——1732).

Pausanias The Betrayer Of His Country. A Tragedy. D.L. late in 1695. 4to. 1696, as " *Written by a Person of Quality.*" This play was introduced to the stage by Southerne, who subscribed the Dedication to Anthony Henly, Esq., Of the *Grange* in *Hampshire.*

O

OLDMIXON, JOHN (1673–1742).

Amintas. A Pastoral. " Made *English* out of *Italian* from the *Aminta* of *Tasso.*" D.L. 1698. 4to. 1698.

The Grove, Or Love's Paradice. An Opera. D.L. 19 February, 1699–1700. 4to. 1700. Advertised *Post Boy,* 16 March, 1699–1700.

The Governour of Cyprus. L.I.F. 1703. 4to, 1703.

OTWAY, THOMAS (1652–1685).

Alcibiades : A Tragedy. D.G. September, 1675. 4tos, 1675 (two editions) ; 1687 ; 8vo, 1777.

Don Carlos Prince of Spain : A Tragedy. D.G. Easter, 1676. Licensed (for printing) 15 June, 1676. 4tos, 1676, 1679, 1686, 1695, 1704 ; 8vo, 1777.

Titus and Berenice. A Tragedy Acted at the Duke's Theatre, With a Farce called the *Cheats of Scapin,* Written in French by Molière : and rendered into English with much Addition and Advantage. D.G. January, 1677. Licensed (for printing) Febr. the 19th, 1676-7. 4tos, 1677, two issues, the first of which omits four lines on p. 17 (leaf C1), but these are inserted on p. 17 (substituted leaf C1) in the second issue ; 1701. 8vo, 1776.

Friendship In Fashion : A Comedy. D.G. April, 1678. Licensed (for printing) 31 May, 1678. 4to, 1678 ; 8vo, 1776.

The History and Fall Of Caius Marius : A Tragedy. D.G. September, 1679. 4tos, 1680, 1692, 1694, 1696, 1703 ; 12mo, 1733 ; 12mo, 1735 ; 8vo, 1777.

The Orphan : Or, The Unhappy-Marriage : A Tragedy. D.G. February, 1680. 4tos, 1680, 1685, 1691, 1696, 1703, 1705 ; 8vo, 1711 ; 16mo, 1711 (Hague) ; 12mo, 1733 ; 12mo, 1735 ; 12mo, 1748 ; 12mo, 1754 ; 12mo, 1759. 16mo, 1769 (Dublin) ; 12mo, 1776 ; 12mo, 1785 ; Dicks, No. 137.

The Souldiers Fortune : A Comedy. D.G. March, 1680. 4tos, 1681, 1683, 1687, 1695. (Upon the title-page 1695 is announced as *The Third Edition,* but it must be the Fourth Quarto.) 12mo. 1735.

Venice Preserv'd, Or, A Plot Discover'd. A Tragedy. D.G. 9th February, 1682. 4tos, 1682, 1696 (two editions) ; 1704 ; 8vo, 1711 ; 12mo, 1728 ; 12mo, 1732 ; 12mo, 1735 ;

12mo (1749); 12mo, 1750. 8vo, 1776; 8vo, n.d. (1790?);
8vo, 1811 (as revised by Kemble); 8vo, 1818. 12mo, 1850;
Dicks, No. 52; 4to, 1885 (Exeter).

The Atheist : Or, The Second Part Of The Souldiers Fortune.
D.L. in the autumn (September–October) of 1683. 4to,
1684; 12mo, 1735.

Heroick Friendship, A Tragedy, by the late Mr. Otway.
4to. 1719. Not acted. A spurious piece.

The Works of Mr. Thomas Otway were collected in one
volume, 4to, 1691. Other editions are : 2 vols., 12mo,
1712 ; 2 vols. 8vo, 1728 ; 2 vols. 8vo, 1736; 3 vols. 8vo,
1757; 3 vols. 12mo, 1768 ; 2 vols. 8vo, 1812 ; 3 vols. 8vo
(by Thomas Thornton), 1813.

The Orphan and *Venice Preserv'd* are included in all the
eighteenth century and later collections of plays, but the
texts often being from the prompt-books are far from
accurate or reliable. In *Sharpe's British Theatre,* Vol. IX,
1804, the text of *The Orphan* is given entire, but passages
are marked with inverted commas, being omitted in contemporary performance. In *The Select London Stage,* one
volume [1824], an abridged text of *The Orphan* is printed.
Venice Preserv'd in particular is mutilated in many late
editions, and the Aquilina scenes are not printed. There is,
however, no uniformity in practice. In Mrs. Inchbald's
British Theatre, Vol. XII, 12mo, 1808, the text is silently but
drastically abbreviated. Aquilina has wholly disappeared.
In R. Cumberland's *British Drama,* Vol. XI, 1817, the text
is complete, but long scenes and separate passages are
marked by inverted commas for omission in the theatre.
In John Cumberland's *British Theatre,* Vol. II, 1829, *Venice
Preserv'd* is " Printed from the Acting Copy." Of Antonio,
Aquilina, and a great deal more beside no vestige remains.

Otway is represented in the *Mermaid Series,* 8vo, 1888,

Vizetelly and Co., by *Don Carlos*, *The Orphan*, *The Souldiers Fortune*, and *Venice Preserv'd*. Introduction by the Hon. Roden Noel.
The Complete Works of Thomas Otway. Edited by Montague Summers. Three Volumes, 4to, 1926.

P

PARKHURST, FERDINANDO.
Ignoramus, or the Academical Lawyer, " acted at the Cockpit in Drury Lane, and also before the King and Queen's Majesty at Whitehall on Saturday night, 1 Nov., 1662." Not printed. M.S. folio, in the library of the Duke of Westminster at Eton Hall, Cheshire.

PAYNE, HENRY NEVIL (1648 ?–1705 ?).
The Fatal Jealousie. A Tragedy. D.G. 3 August, 1672. Licensed November 22, 1672. 4to. 1673. (T.C. 6 May, 1673.)
The Morning Ramble, Or, The Town-Humours. D.G. 4 November, 1672. 4to. 1673. (T.C. 6 May, 1673.)
The Siege of Constantinople. A Tragedy. D.G. 2 November, 1674. 4to. 1675. (T.C. 15 February, 1675.)

PENKETHMAN (PINKETHMAN), WILLIAM (——1725).
Love without Interest : Or, The Man too hard for the Master. A Comedy. D.L. 1699. 4to. 1699.

PERRIN, PIERRE (?——1680).
Ariadne, Or, The Marriage of Bacchus. An Opera, Or A Vocal Representation. *First Compos'd by Monsieur* P. P. Now put into Musick by Monsieur *Grabut*, Master of His Majesties *Musick*. And Acted by the Royall Academy Of Musick, At The *Theatre-Royal* in *Covent-Garden*. D.L. March, 1674. 4to. 1673-4. *Ariane, ou le Mariage de Bacchus* was first given at Issy in 1661.

PHILIPS, *Mrs.* KATHERINE (1632–1664).

Pompey. A Tragedy. Smock Alley, Dublin. 10 February, 1662–3. 4to. Dublin, 1663. (S.R. 15 Feb. 1663–4.)
Pompey. A Tragoedy. 4to. London, 1663, as "Acted with Great Applause." In *Poems.* By The Incomparable Mrs. K. P., folio, London, 1664. In *Poems.* By the most deservedly Admired Mrs. Katherine Philips The Matchless Orinda, folio, 1667; 1669; 1678; 8vo, 1710.

Horace. A Tragedy. Translated from Monsieur Corneille. Mrs. Philips only Englished as far as Act IV, Scene VI. In the *Poems,* folio, 1667 (pp. 67–112). The play was completed by Sir John Denham, and thus was given at D.L., January, 1667. The piece was then printed in the *Poems* of Katherine Philips, folio, 1669 and 1678. Tonson, however, in the 8vo 1710, wishing to place the French original on the opposite page, substituted Charles Cotton's version as superior to that of Denham.

PHILIPS, WILLIAM.

The Revengeful Queen : A Tragedy. D.L. 1698. 4to 1698.

Alcamenes and Menalippa. A Tragedy. Ascribed to William Philips by Mears.

PIX, *Mrs.* MARY, *née* GRIFFITH (1666–1709).

The Spanish Wives. A Farce. D.L. September, 1696. 4to. 1696 (two issues). (T.C. Nov. 1696.)

Ibrahim The Thirteenth Emperour Of The Turks : A Tragedy. D.L. 1696. 4to. 1696.

The Innocent Mistress. A Comedy. L.I.F. July, 1697. Publication announced " this day " in the *Post Boy,* 29–31 July, 1697. (T.C. November, 1697.)

The Deceiver Deceived : A Comedy. L.I.F. October, 1697.

Publication announced " this day " in the *Post Boy*, 18–21 Dec., 1697. 4to. 1698. The music was by Finger.

The French Beau : A Comedy. Acted by His Majesty's Servants At The New Theatre in Little-Lincoln's-Inn-Fields. 4to. 1699. This is *The Deceiver Deceived* with the title-page and three succeeding leaves cancelled. A new title is substituted, as also one leaf carrying *recto* a new Prologue, *verso* " Persons Represented," a list with the names of three additional actors and several further variants.

Queen Catharine Or, The Ruines of Love. A Tragedy. L.I.F. September, 1698. 4to. 1698. (T.C. Nov., 1698.)

The False Friend, Or the Fate of Disobedience. A Tragedy. L.I.F. 1699. 4to, 1699 ; 4to, 1702.

The Beau Defeated ; Or, The Lucky Younger Brother. A Comedy. L.I.F. February, 1699–1700. Published, *Post Boy*, 18 April, 1700. 4to, n.d. [1700].

The Double Distress. A Tragedy. L.I.F. January, 1700–1. 4to. 1701. Advertised *Post Man*, 3 April, 1701. The title-page carries an advertisement : " Next Week will be Published *The Czar of Muscovy.* A Tragedy, Printed for B. Lintott."

The Czar of Muscovy. A Tragedy. L.I.F. February, 1700–1701. Publication advertised *Post Boy*, 15 April, 1701. 4to. 1701.

The Different Widows : Or, Intrigue All-A-Mode. A Comedy. L.I.F. October, 1703. 4to, n.d. [1703]. (T.C. Dec., 1703.)

The Conquest of Spain : A Tragedy. Haymarket : " the beginning of *May*, 1705." (Downes.) 4to. 1705. (T.C. May, 1705.)

The Adventures In Madrid. A Comedy. Haymarket, July, 1706. 4to, n.d. [1706]. (Published 10 August, 1706.)

PORDAGE, SAMUEL (1633–1692 ?).

Troades Englished. By S. P. Unacted. 12mo. 1660. In *Poems Upon Several Occasions.* By S. P. Gent. 12mo. 1660. " *Troades.* A Tragedy Written in Latine By *Lucius Annæus Seneca :* Translated Into our Vernacular Tongue."

Herod And Mariamne : A Tragedy. D.G. October, 1673. (S.R. 18 Feb., 1673–4.) 4to. 1673. The Prologue has " Spoken at the Theatre in *Lincolns-Inn-Fields.*" The tragedy, however, was a Dorset Garden production, and the title-page has " Acted at the Duke's Theatre." The Dedication to the Duchess of Albemarle is signed by Elkanah Settle.

The practice of printing quite other prologues with plays was by no means uncommon. Many examples might be cited. Thus Ravenscroft printed a D.G. prologue with his T.R. *Titus Andronicus.* 4to. 1687.

The Siege of Babylon. D.G. autumn of 1677. Licensed Nov. 2, 1677. 4to. 1678.

PORTER, THOMAS (1636–1680).

The Villain. A Tragedy. L.I.F. October, 1662. (S.R. 15 June, 1663.) 4to, 1663 ; 4tos, 1670, 1694.

The Witty Combat : Or, The Female Victor. A Trage-Comedy. "As It was *Acted* by Persons of Quality in *Whitson*-Week with great applause." In the year 1663 Whit Sunday fell on 7 June. (This piece is not to be identified with *The German Princess* seen by Pepys, 15 April, 1664, at L.I.F.) 4to. 1663. " Written by T. P. Gent."

The Carnival. A Comedy. D.L. 1663. 4to. 1664.

The French Conjurer. D.G. spring of 1677. 4to. 1678. Licensed for printing August 2, 1677. (T.C. Michaelmas, 26 November, 1677.)

POWELL, GEORGE (1659–1714).

The Treacherous Brothers. A Tragedy. D.G. first week of February, 1689–90. (S.R. 13 Feb., 1689–90.) 4to, 1690; 4tos, 1696 (T.C. May, 1696), 1699.

Alphonso King Of Naples. A Tragedy. D.L. December, 1690. 4to. 1691. (T.C. Feb., 1691.)

A Very Good Wife. A Comedy. D.L. 1692–3. 4to, 1693 (T.C. Nov., 1693); 4to, 1703.

Bonduca : Or, The British Heroine. A Tragedy. " With a New Entertainment of Musick, *Vocal* and *Instrumental.*" D.L. September, 1695. First Edition advertised *London Gazette*, 24–28 October, 1695. 4to. 1696. (T.C. June, 1696.) Music by Henry Purcell.

The Cornish Comedy. D.G. June, 1696. Advertised *Post Boy*, 25–27 August, 1696. 4to. 1696.

A New Opera ; Called, Brutus of Alba : Or, Augusta's Triumph. D.G. September, 1696. 4to. 1697. The Dedication to Briscoe signed, George Powell, Jack Verbruggen, is dated Monday, 16 October, 1696.

The Imposture Defeated : Or, A Trick to Cheat the Devil. A Comedy. D.L. August, 1697. 4to. 1698. Advertised as " published this day," *Post Boy*, 16–18 Nov., 1697. (T.C. Nov., 1697; Feb., 1698; May, 1698, as *Impostor defeated*.)

R

RAVENSCROFT, EDWARD (1643/4–1707).

The Citizen Turn'd Gentleman. D.G. 4 July, 1672. Licensed August 9th, 1672. 4to. 1672. (T.C. 21 November, 1672.) This comedy was reissued, 4to, 1675 (T.C. 24 November, 1675), as *Mamamouchi ; Or The Citizen Turn'd Gentleman.*

The Careless Lovers.   A Comedy.   D.G. first week in March, 1672–3.   4to.   1673.   (T.C. 24 November, 1673, as *The Careless Lovers, or The Conceited Travellers.*)

The Wrangling Lovers : Or, The Invisible Mistress.   A Comedy.   D.G. September, 1676.   Licensed Sept. 25th, 1676.   4to.   1677.   (T.C. 24 November, 1676.)   This 4to was issued with two separate title-pages.   In each case *recto* is identical, but in A, *verso* carries L'Estrange's license and no list of errata ; in B, *verso* carries no license, but an incorrect list of errata.

Scaramouch A Philosopher, Harlequin A School-Boy, Bravo, Merchant, and Magician.   A Comedy After the Italian manner. D.L. 5 May, 1677.   4to.   1677.   (T.C. 5 July, 1677.)

King Edgar And Alfreda.   A Tragi-Comedy.   D.L. October, 1677.   Advertised in *The London Gazette,* 29 Oct.– 1 Nov., 1677.   4to.   1677.   (T.C. 28 February, 1678.)

The English Lawyer.   A Comedy.   D.L. December, 1677. 4to.   1678.   (T.C. 14 May, 1678.)   Dublin, 8vo, 1737. (As *Ignoramus ; or, The English Lawyer,* London, 12mo, 1736 ; Dublin, 12mo, n.d., 1720 ?.)

Titus Andronicus, Or The Rape of Lavinia.   A Tragedy, Alter'd from *Mr. Shakespears* Works.   D.L. winter of 1679. Licensed (for printing) December 21, 1686.   4to.   1687. (T.C. 28 February, 1687.)

The London Cuckolds.   A Comedy.   D.G. November, 1681. 4to.   1682.   (T.C. Feb., 1682.)   4to, 1688, 1697 ; 12mo, 1734.   Reprinted in *Restoration Comedies,* Edited by Montague Summers, 1921.

Dame Dobson : Or, The Cunning Woman.   A Comedy. D.G. 1 June, 1683.   4to.   1684.   (T.C. Nov., 1683.)

The Canterbury Guests ; Or, A Bargain Broken.   A Comedy. D.L. September, 1694.   (Publication advertised in *The London Gazette,* 17–20 December, 1694.)   4to.   1695.

The Anatomist : Or, The Sham Doctor. Written by Mr. *Ravenscroft*. With *The Loves Of Mars and Venus*. A Play Set to Music, Written by Mr. *Motteux* As they are Acted together. L.I.F. 14 November, 1696. 4to, 1697; 12mo, 1722; 12mo, 1735; 8vo, 1762; 8vo, 1777; 12mo, 1784; 12mo, 1786. Reduced to a farce of one act, with the Play Set to Music as written by Motteux omitted *The Anatomist* was printed, 8vo, n d. [*c.* 1744], and 12mo, 1763. It is thus included in *Sharpe's British Theatre*, Vol. XIII, 1805.

The Italian Husband. A Tragedy. L.I.F. autumn of 1697. (Dedicatory Epistle dated, London, Decemb. 16, 1697.) 4to. 1698. Advertised in *Post Boy*, 16–18 December, 1697, as "published yesterday." The music was composed by Eccles.

RAWLINS, THOMAS (1620 ?–1670).
The Rebellion : A Tragedy : As it was acted nine dayes together, and divers times since with good applause, by his Majesties Company of Revells. Acted at Blackfriars, 1639. 4to. 1640.

RAWLINS, ——.
Tom Essence : Or, The Modish Wife. A Comedy. D.G. September, 1676. Licensed Novemb. the 4th, 1676. 4to. 1677. This comedy is anonymous, but is ascribed by Langbaine to " One Mr. *Rawlins*," who has been confused with the author of *The Rebellion*.

Tunbridge-Wells : Or A Days Courtship. A Comedy. Written by a Person of Quality. D.G. February–March, 1678. 4to. 1678. " I have been told it was writ by Mr. *Rawlins* " : Langbaine.

REVET, EDWARD.
The Town-Shifts, Or, The Suburb-Justice : A Comedy. L.I.F. March, 1671. Licensed May 2, 1671. 4to. 1671.

The title-page does not give the author's name, but the Epistle Dedicatory to Stephen Mosedelf, Esq., is signed Edw. Revet.

RHODES, RICHARD (?–1668).
 Flora's Vagaries. A Comedy. T.R., Vere Street, January, 1663. (S.R. 4 Feb., 1663–4.) Licensed July 28, 1669. 4to, 1670 ; 4to, 1677.

This comedy was acted by amateurs (undergraduates) at Christ Church, Oxford, 8 January, 1663, and was given professionally in London at the Theatre Royal, Vere Street, either that same month or very early in the following February. The performance recorded by Herbert, 3 November, 1663, cannot be the first in London, as Prospero was originally played by Theophilus Bird, who died not later than early April, 1663.

LA ROCHE-GUILHEN, *Madame.*
 Rare en Tout. Comedie meslée de musique et de Balets represantée devant sa Majesté sur le Theatre Royal de Whitehall. 4to. 1677. Acted at Court in May, 1677.

RYMER, THOMAS (1641–1713).
 Edgar, Or the English Monarch ; An Heroick Tragedy. Unacted. Licensed *Septemb.* 13, 1677. (T.C. 26 Nov., 1677.) 4to, 1678 ; 4to, 1691 ; as *The English Monarch.* 4to, 1693.

S

S., T.
 Youth's Comedy Or The Souls Tryals And Triumph ; " A Dramatick Poem With Divers Meditations intermixt upon several Subjects. Set forth to Help and Encourage those that are seeking a HEAVENLY COUNTREY " (not intended to

be acted).   8vo.   1680.   " To The Reader, Especially The Younger Sort," signed T. S.

SACKVILLE, CHARLES, *sixth* EARL *of* DORSET, *and first* EARL *of* MIDDLESEX (1638–1706).
   Pompey the Great.   A Tragedy.   As it was Acted by the Servants of His Royal Highness the Duke of York.   Translated out of French by Certain Persons of Honour.   L.I.F. December, 1663.   Also acted at Whitehall.   4to.   1664, Sackville translated the last Act of this play from Corneille's *La Mort de Pompée.*

SADLER, ANTHONY (1610–1685 ?).
   The Subjects Joy For the Kings Restoration, Cheerfully made known in A Sacred Masque : Gratefully made publique For His Sacred Majesty.   By the Author of *Inquisitio Anglicana.*   Unacted.   4to.   1660.   Headlines, *A Divine Masque.*

SAINT-EVREMOND, CHARLES DE SAINT-DENIS-LE-GUAST, SEIGNEUR DE (1613–1703).
   Sir Politick Would-Be, Comedie A la manière des Anglois. Not acted.   Printed in *Oeuvres Meslees* De Mr· De Saint-Evremond, . . . A   Londres,   Chez   Jacob   Tonson. M.DCC.IX.   (Seconde Edition.)   3 tomes, 4to.   Tome I. pp. 251–348.

ST. SERFE, THOMAS.
   Tarugo's Wiles : Or, The Coffee-House.   L.I.F. 5 October, 1667.   4to.   1668.   St. Serfe is sometimes termed Sir Thomas St. Serfe, but the title is doubtful.   To him also has been ascribed *Marciana or The Discovery,* for which see under WILLIAM CLARK.

SAUNDERS, CHARLES (1663–1684).
Tamerlane The Great. A Tragedy. D.L. February, 1681.
4to. 1681. (T.C. May, 1681.)

SCOTT, THOMAS (1674–?).
The Mock-Marriage. A Comedy. D.G., during the first
week of October, 1695. (Advertised in *The London Gazette*,
10–14 Oct., 1695.) 4to. 1696.
The Unhappy Kindness : Or A Fruitless Revenge. A
Tragedy. D.L. July, 1697. 4to. 1697.

SEDLEY, *Sir* CHARLES (1639–1701).
Pompey the Great. A Tragedy. As it was Acted by the
Servants of His Royal Highness the Duke of York. Trans-
lated out of French by Certain Persons of Honour. L.I.F.
December, 1663. Also acted at Whitehall. 4to. 1664.
Sir Charles Sedley translated one act of this play from
Corneille's *La Mort de Pompée.*
The Mulberry-Garden. A Comedy. D.L. 18 May, 1668.
4to. 1668. 4tos, 1675, 1688. Originally named *The
Wandering Ladys.*
Antony And Cleopatra : A Tragedy. D.G. February,
1676–7. (S.R. 4 May, 1677.) Licensed Apr. 24, 1677.
4to. 1677. (T.C. 28 May, 1677.) 4to. 1696.
Bellamira, Or The Mistress, A Comedy : D.L. 12 May,
1687. Licensed May 24, 1687. (S.R. 17 June, 1687.) 4to.
1687.
Beauty the Conqueror or the Death of Marc Antony. In
*Miscellaneous Works Of the Honourable Sir Charles Sedley, Bar*ᵗ
8vo. 1702. A version made by Sedley of his *Antony and
Cleopatra,* recast as a classical tragedy with choruses between
the acts. It seems to have been unfinished, and is printed
in an incomplete form.

The Grumbler : A Comedy Of Three Acts. Never Before Printed. *London,* printed 1719. First printed with separate title-page in Briscoe's edition of Sedley's *Works,* 2 vols., 12mo, 1722 ; vol. II. *The Grumbler* was adapted for the stage by Garrick in April, 1754, and again by Goldsmith for Quick's benefit, 8 May, 1773. *The Grumbler* is a fairly close translation of *Le Grondeur,* by Brueys and Palaprat.

The Tyrant King of Crete. A Tragedy. 12mo. 1722. In Briscoe's edition of Sedley's *Works,* 2 vols., 12mo, 1722 ; vol. II. An abbreviated version of Henry Killigrew's *Pallantus and Eudora,* folio, 1653.

The Miscellaneous Works Of the Honourable Sir Charles Sedley, Bar^t : 8vo, 1702, contains (and it is the first edition of) *Beauty the Conqueror. The Works of the Honourable Sir Charles Sedley, Bar^t* : 2 vols., 12mo, 1722, contains (and is the first edition of) *The Tyrant King of Crete. Works,* 2 vols., 8vo, 1776 ; *Works,* 2 vols., 12mo, 1778. *The Poetical and Dramatic Works of Sir Charles Sedley,* edited by V. de Sola Pinto. Two volumes, 1928. *Pompey the Great, Beauty the Conqueror,* and *The Tyrant King of Crete* are omitted.

SETTLE, ELKANAH (1648–1724).

Cambyses King of Persia : A Tragedy. L.I.F. January, 1670–1. Licensed March 6, 1670[–1]. 4to. 1671. (T.C. 30 May, 1671.) 4tos, 1672, 1672, 1675, 1692.

The Empress of Morocco. A Tragedy. D.G. 3 July, 1673. 4to. 1673. " The Empress of Morocco. A Tragedy With Sculptures." Frontispiece, Exterior Duke's House ; and five copper plates illustrating the play. (T.C. 24 November, 1673.) Another issue, 4to, 1673 ; 4tos, 1687, 1698. Edited by Montague Summers, 1935.

Love And Revenge. A Tragedy. D.G. 9 November, 1674.

4to. 1675. (T.C. 10 May, 1675.) MS. in Settle's hand. B.M., Harleian 6903.

The Conquest of China, By the Tartars. A Tragedy. D.G. 20 May, 1675. 4to. 1676. (T.C. 10 Feb., 1676.)

Ibrahim The Illustrious Bassa. A Tragedy. D.G. March, 1676. (S.R. 7 July, 1676.) Licensed May the 4th, 1676. 4to. 1677. (T.C. 22 Nov. 1676.) 4to. 1694.

Pastor Fido : Or, The Faithful Shepherd. A Pastoral. D.G. December, 1676. (S.R. 22 Jan., 1676–7.) Licensed Decemb. the 26th, 1676. 4to. 1677. (T.C. 5 July, 1677.) 4tos, 1689, 1694. MS. Bodley. Rawl. Poet. 8. There is a broadside Prologue, " Spoken by *Mr. Edward Lambert,*" and Epilogue, " Spoken by *Sir Walter Ernle* Baronet," to an amateur performance given in 1686.

The Female Prelate : Being The History of the Life and Death Of Pope Joan. A Tragedy. D.L. July, 1679. 4to. 1680. (T.C. Nov., 1680.) Second edition as by " A Person of Quality," and without the Dedication to Shaftesbury, 4to, 1689.

As this has erroneously been said to be a re-issue it may be worth while pointing out that such is not the case. The text has been entirely reset, and there are variants, unimportant in themselves but fairly numerous. Edited by Montague Summers, 1935.

Fatal Love : Or, The Forc'd Inconstancy. A Tragedy. D.L. September, 1680. 4to. 1680. (T.C. Nov. 1680.)

The Heir Of Morocco, With The Death of Gayland. A Tragedy. D.L. 11th March, 1682. 4to. 1682. (T.C. May, 1682.)

Distress'd Innocence : Or, The Princess of Persia. A Tragedy. D.L. November, 1690. Publication announced in *The London Gazette*, 11–15 Dec., 1690. 4to. 1691. (T.C. Feb., 1691.)

The Fairy-Queen. An Opera. D.G. April, 1692. Publication announced in *The London Gazette*, May 5–9, 1692. (S.R., *The Fayery Queene, or Midsomers Nights Dreame*, 2 Nov., 1691.) 4to. 1692. "With Alterations, Additions, and several New Songs," 4to, 1693.

The evidence for attribution to Settle is argued in detail by F. C. Brown, *Elkanah Settle*, 1910 ; but it remains doubtful.

The New Athenian Comedy, Containing, The Politicks, Oeconomicks, Tacticks, Crypticks, Apocalypticks, Stypticks, Scepticks, Pneumaticks, Theologicks, Poeticks, Mathematicks, Sophisticks, Pragmaticks, Dogmaticks, &c. Of that most Learned Society. Unacted. A Satire in three acts. 4to. 1693.

The Ambitious Slave ; Or, A Generous Revenge. A Tragedy. D.L. February, 1693–4. 4to. 1694.

Philaster : Or, Love lies a bleeding. A Tragi-Comedy. "Revis'd, and the Two last Acts new Written." D.L. late in 1695. 4to. 1695. (T.C. June Trinity, 1696.)

The World in the Moon : An Opera. D.G. 17 June, 1697. 4to. 1697. (T.C. Published Wednesday, 23 June, 1697.) *Post Boy*, No. 333, 22–24 June, 1697. *Post Boy*, 29 June— 1 July, 1697, advertises : "The New Opera, called The *World in the Moon* is Acting with great Applause. It is Licensed by the Lord Chamberlain's Secretary and the Master of the Revels." Second Edition, 4to, 1697. Advertised in *Post Boy*, 28–31 August, 1697.

The single songs in the New Opera of *The World in the Moon.* Set by Dr. [Daniel] Purcell and Mr. [Jeremiah] Clarke. Price 6*d.* (T.C. June, 1697.)

The Virgin Prophetess : Or, The Fate of Troy. An Opera. D.L. 15 May, 1701. 4to, 1701 ; 4to, 1702, as, *Cassandra Or The Virgin Prophetesse. The Musical Entertainments In*

The Virgin Prophetess : Or, The Fate of Troy. A New Opera.
Perform'd at the Theatre Royal. Composed by Mr.
Finger. 4to. 1701. The libretto, but not the score.

The Siege of Troy. A Tragi-Comedy. A Droll, acted at
the Fairs, and first presented by Mrs. Minns in her Great
Booth at Bartholomew Fair, 22–25 August, 1703 ; and
again at Southwark Fair, which continued for a fortnight
in September. *The Siege of Troy* is actually the play which
is being given in Hogarth's picture of " Southwark Fair,"
painted in 1733. *The Siege of Troy* was very popular. In
September, 1724, it was given at Southwark Fair at the
Booths of Lee and Harper ; in 1747 at Bartholomew Fair
and Southwark Fair by Lee, Yeates, and Warner. This
little piece was printed 12mo, 1703 : THE NEW HISTORY
OF THE TROJAN WARS AND *TROY'S* DESTRUC-
TION. To which is added the Siege of Troy, a Tragi-
Comedy, as it has been often acted with great Applause."
This became a favourite chap-book, and there were number-
less editions throughout the eighteenth century. 12mo,
1707, 1708, 1715, 1716. (1715 and 1716 describe *The Siege
of Troy* as " A Dramatic Performance, Presented in Mrs.
Mynn's Great Booth, in the Queen's-Arms-Yard near the
Marshalsea-Gate in *Southwark*, during the Time of the Fair.")
12mo, 1718, 1728, 1751 ; with general title-page *The Siege
of Troy*, A Tragi-Comedy. Berwick, 8vo, 1791. This list
does not intend to be complete, but is merely indicative of
the frequent reprints.

St. George for England. A Droll. Acted at Bartholomew
Fair. Not Printed. One Droll of this name was acted at
the Fair in August, 1688.

The City-Ramble : Or, A Play-House Wedding. A Comedy.
D.L. 17 August, 1711. 4to, n.d. [1711].

The Lady's Triumph. A Comi-Dramatic Opera. L.I.F.

22 March, 1718. 12mo. 1718. A MS. prompt-book of this Opera is preserved in the Bodleian Library ; MS. Rawl. Poet. 136. See *The Restoration Theatre*, 1934, by Montague Summers, pp. 142–3 ; and p. 80, facing which a leaf of the MS. is reproduced.

The Expulsion of the Danes from Britain. A Tragedy. Not Printed. The *Biographia Dramatica*, 1812, Vol. I, Part I, p. 641, says that some months before Settle's decease he offered this play to the managers of the Theatre Royal in Drury Lane, but he lived not to bring it on the stage. The MS. has not been traced.

Pageants :

The Triumphs of London.   4to.   1691.
The Triumphs of London.   4to.   1692.
The Triumphs of London.   4to.   1693.
The Triumphs of London.   4to.   1694.
The Triumphs of London.   4to.   1695.
Glory's Resurrection ; Being the Triumphs of London Revived.
    folio, 1698.
The Triumphs of London.   folio.   1699.
The Triumphs of London.   folio.   1700.
The Triumphs of London.   folio.   1701.
The Triumphs of London.   folio.   1702.
The Triumphs of London.   folio.   1708.   This pageantry was never displayed, since Prince George of Denmark died on the 28 October, the day before the intended exhibition, and the Lord Mayor, Sir Charles Duncombe, entered on his office without the usual show.

Elkanah Settle was also the chief engineer and mechanician of the Pope-burning pageants, which took place on 17 November, in the years 1679, 1680, and 1681.

SHADWELL, THOMAS. *Poet Laureate.* (1641–1692).

The Sullen Lovers : Or, The Impertinents. A Comedy. L.I.F. 2 May, 1668. (S.R. 9 Sept., 1668). 4to. 1668. (T.C. November, 1668.) 4tos, 1670, 1693.

The Royal Shepherdess. A Tragi-Comedy. L.I.F. 25 February, 1668–9. (S.R. 8 June, 1669.) 4to. 1669. (T.C. 22 Nov., 1669.) 4to. 1691.

The Hypocrite. L.I.F. Probably a version from Molière's *Tartuffe*, produced early in 1670 to forestall Medbourne's *Tartuffe* given at Drury Lane in the Lent of this year. Not Printed. References in Settle's Preface to *Ibrahim The Illustrious Bassa,* 4to, 1677 ; and in *Mac Flecknoe.*

The Humorists. A Comedy. L.I.F. December, 1670. (S.R. 9 February, 1670–1.) 4to. 1671. (T.C. 30 May, 1671.)

The Miser. A Comedy. D.L. January, 1671–2. 4to. 1672. (T.C. 24 June 1672.) 4to. 1691.

Epsom-Wells. A Comedy. D.G. 2 December, 1672. (S.R. 17 Feb., 1672–3.) Licensed Feb. 17, 1673-4. 4to. 1673. (T.C. 6 May, 1673.) 4tos, 1676, 1693, 1704.

The Tempest, Or The Enchanted Island. A Comedy. Shadwell's operatic version of the Davenant and Dryden comedy. D.G. 30 April, 1674. 4to. 1674. (T.C. 25 Nov., 1674.) 4tos, 1676, two issues ; 1690 ; 1695 ; 1701. And in the various collected editions of Dryden, 12mo, 1717, 1735 ; 8vo, 1762 ; erroneously as the Davenant and Dryden comedy.

Psyche. A Tragedy. D.G. 27 February, 1674–5. (S.R. 1 Aug., 1674.) 4to. 1675. (T.C. 15 Feb., 1675.) 4to. 1690.

The Libertine : A Tragedy. D.G. June, 1675. 4to. 1676. (T.C. 10 Feb., 1676.) 4tos, 1697, 1704, 1705.

The Virtuoso. A Comedy. D.G. May, 1676. (S.R.

23 Feb., 1677–8.)   4to.   1676.   Licensed May 31, 1676.
4tos, 1691, 1704.

The History Of Timon of Athens, The Man-Hater.   Made
into a Play.   D.G. December, 1677 ; or January, 1677–78.
(S.R. 23 Feb. 1677–78.)   4to.   1678.   Licensed Feb. 18,
1677-8.   4tos, 1680, 1688, 1696, 1703.

A True Widow.   A Comedy.   D.G. December, 1678.
4to.   1679.   (T.C. May, 1679.)   The First Quarto was
reissued with a new title-page, dated 1689, and a new final
page carrying the Epilogue.

The Woman-Captain.   A Comedy.   D.G. September, 1679.
4to.   1680.   (T.C. November, 1679.)

*The Lancashire Witches, And Teague o Divelly The Irish
Priest :*   A Comedy.   After considerable delay produced
at Dorset Garden in the autumn (probably September) of
1681.   4to.   1682.   (T.C. Nov. 1681.)   " Printed as it
was intended (but not allowed) to be acted."   Second
Edition, 4to, 1682 ; 4to, 1691 ; 12mo, 1736.

In 1853 James Halliwell issued (80 copies for Private
Circulation only) *The Poetry of Witchcraft Illustrated by
Copies of the Plays on The Lancashire Witches by Heywood and
Shadwell.*   The text is very poor and inaccurate, and there
is no attempt at annotation.

The Squire of Alsatia.   A Comedy.   D.L. 4 May, 1688.
4to.   1688.   (T.C. May, 1688.)   4tos, 1692, 1693, 1699.
12mo, 1715 ; 12mo, Dublin 1735 ; 8vo, Dublin, 1738.
This play was originally to have been named *The Alsatia
Bully.*

Bury-Fair.   A Comedy.   D.L. April, 1689.   4to.   1689.
(T.C. June, 1689.)

*The Amorous Bigotte : With The Second Part Of Teague
O Divelly.*   A Comedy.   D.L. 1689–90.   4to.   1690.   (T.C.
May, 1690.)

The Scowrers.   A Comedy.   D.L. December, 1690.   4to.
1691.   (T.C. February, 1691.)

The Volunteers, Or The Stock-Jobbers.   A Comedy.   D.L.
last week of November or first week of December, 1692.
4to.   1693.   (T.C. June, 1693.)

The Works Of Tho. Shadwell, Esq ; 17 plays with general
title-page, 1693.   The quartos, some first, some later, bound
together in one volume.   *The Tempest* is omitted.   For full
bibliographical details and a facsimile of the title-page see
my edition of *Shadwell,* 1927, Vol. 1, pp. XI–XIII.

The Dramatick Works of Thomas Shadwell.   Four Volumes.
12mo.   1720.

The Complete Works of Thomas Shadwell.   Edited by
Montague Summers.   Five Volumes.   4to.   1927.

SHERBURNE, *Sir* EDWARD (1618–1702).

Medea.   Unacted.   8vo.   1648 ; 8vo, 1701.

Troades   Unacted.   8vo.   1679.   Publication advertised
in *The London Gazette,* 10–14 July, 1679.   8vo.   1701.

Phaedra and Hippolitus.   Unacted.   8vo.   1701.

SHIPMAN, THOMAS (1632–1680).

Henry The Third Of France, Stabb'd by a Fryer.   *With The
Fall of the Guise.*   A Tragedy.   Originally produced by
Killigrew's company at Lincoln's Inn Fields between
Easter 1672 and 1673.   Revived June 1678, at the Theatre
Royal.   Licensed Octob. 16, 1678.   Roger L'Estrange.
4to.   1678.   (T.C. Michaelmas, 6 December, 1678.)

SMITH, HENRY.

The Princess of Parma.   A Tragedy.   L.I.F.   1698–9.
4to.   1699.

SMITH, JOHN (*c.* 1620–1683).
Cytherea : Or The Enamouring Girdle. A New Comedy. Written by *John Smith* of *Snenton* in *York-shire*, Gent. Licensed May 30, 1677. Unacted. 4to. 1677.

SOUTHBY,——.
Timoleon : Or, The Revolution. A Tragi-Comedy. 4to 1697. (Apparently unacted.)

SOUTHERNE, THOMAS (1660–1746).
The Loyal Brother, Or, The Persian Prince. A Tragedy. D.L. 7th February, 1682. 4to. 1682.
The Disappointment, Or The Mother in Fashion. A Play. D.L. 5 April, 1684. 4to. 1684.
Sir Anthony Love : Or, The Rambling Lady. A Comedy. D.L. November, 1690. Advertised in *The London Gazette*, 19–22 December, 1690. 4to. 1691. 4to, 1698, as *Sir Antony Love : Or, The Rambling Lady.*
The Wives Excuse ; Or, Cuckolds Make Themselves. A Comedy. D.L. December, 1691. 4to, 1692. (T.C. February, 1692.) 12mo, 1726.
The Maids last Prayer : Or, Any rather than Fail. A Comedy. D.L. January, 1692–3. Advertised " This day was Published," *London Gazette*, 9–13 March, 1693. 4to. 1693.
The Fatal Marriage : Or The Innocent Adultery. A Play. D.L. February, 1693–4. Advertised, *London Gazette*, 19th–22nd March, 1693–4. 4to, 1694. 8vo, 1719. 12mo, 1732 ; 1735.
Garrick's version of *The Fatal Marriage* was produced at Drury Lane on 2nd December, 1757, and printed 8vo, 1758. Actually the play was not generally spoken of as *Isabella* until some years later. In nearly all the subsequent

collections, Southerne's *The Fatal Marriage* is replaced by Garrick's *Isabella*, frequently under Southerne's name.

Oroonoko : A Tragedy.   D.L. November, 1695.   Advertised *Post Boy*, 16th December, 1695, 4to, 1696 ; 4to, 1699, " The Second Edition " ; 4to, 1699 (another, The Third Edition) ; 12mo, 1711 ; 1712 ; 1721 ; 1722 ; 1735 ; 1736 ; n.d. (1739) ;   1740 ;   1744 ;   1749 ;   1750 ;   1751 ;   1756 ; 1759 ; 8vo, 1777 ; Dicks No. 122.   In *The New English Theatre*, Vol. VI, 1776 ; in R. Cumberland's *British Drama*, Vol. XI, 1817.   Cumberland in his Critique observes that in *Oroonoko* " there are whole scenes, characters and descriptions . . . which the decent manners of the modern stage, after attempting to reform in part, has at length been obliged to expunge in whole."   Many later editions of Southerne's tragedy are grossly mutilated.

Hawkesworth's alteration of *Oroonoko* was first printed, 8vo, 1759 ; another version, 8vo, 1760 ; Francis Gentleman's adaptation, 12mo, 1760, Printed at Glasgow.   Acted at Edinburgh.

In *Sharpe's British Theatre*, Vol. XI, 1805, the text of *Oroonoko* (with separate title-page, 1804) is given entire, but in Mrs. Inchbald's *British Theatre*, Vol. VII, 1808, the text is reduced to a minimum, four characters and a good half of the play have totally disappeared, the Widow Lackitt is deprived of her name and allowed only seven short speeches in Act I, scene 2, after which she vanishes, whilst new dialogue of a very poor quality is written in, not merely to serve as a connecting link, but actually even to commence the play.

It is worth remark that in *A Companion to the Theatre : Or, A View of our most celebrated Dramatic Pieces : in which the Plan, Characters, and Incidents of each are particularly explained*, London, 1747, the plots of *The Fatal Marriage*, pp. 128–136, and of *Oroonoko*, pp. 225–232, are given in full, and in *The Fatal Marriage* the Comedy with the episodes of Fernando, Fabian, Frederick and Victoria, is described at length, whilst in *Oroonoko* an equal attention is given to the Widow Lackitt, the sisters Weldon, and their matrimonial intrigues.

The Fate of Capua. A Tragedy. L.I.F. April, 1700. Advertised in *The London Gazette*, and *Post Man*, 29 April, 1700. 4to. 1700.

The Spartan Dame. A Tragedy. D.L. 11th December, 1719. 8vo. 1719 (three editions); 8vo, 1725 (Dublin).

Money the Mistress. A Play. L.I.F. 19th February, 1726. 8vo. 1726. A MS. prompt book of *Money the Mistress* is preserved in the Bodleian Library; MS. Rawl. Poet. 136. See *The Restoration Theatre* by Montague Summers, 1934, pp. 142–43.

The Works of Mr. Thomas Southerne, 2 vols., 12mo, 1713; this does not, of course, include *The Spartan Dame* and *Money the Mistress*.

The Works of Mr. Thomas Southerne, 2 Vols., 12mo, 1721; (without *Money the Mistress*). *Plays Written by Thomas Southerne, Esq.*, Now First Collected, 3 vols., 12mo, 1774; Printed for T. Evans. The present writer has in preparation an edition of Southerne.

SOUTHLAND, THOMAS.

Love a la Mode. A Comedy. As it was lately [1662] Acted with great Applause at *Middlesex-House*. Written by a Person of Honour. 4to. 1663. " To the Reader " is signed T.S., and Halliwell was certainly right in his ascription of this comedy to Thomas Southland, *Dictionary of Old English Plays*, 1860, p. 150.

Edward Browne in his Memorandum Book, British Museum, MS. Sloane, 1900, notes that he saw *Love a la Mode* at Middlesex House.

The Ungrateful Favourite. A Tragedy. Unacted. Licensed May 11th, 1664. 4to. 1664. " Written By a Person of Honour," who was almost certainly Thomas Southland.

STAPYLTON, *Sir* ROBERT (1599–1669).
The Royal Choice. (S.R. 29th November, 1653.) Not Printed.
The Slighted Maid. A Comedy. L.I.F. February, 1663. (S.R. 14 April, 1663.) 4to. 1663.
The Step-Mother. A Tragi-Comedy. L.I.F. November, 1663. (S.R. 26 Dec., 1663.) 4to. 1664.
The Tragedie Of Hero and Leander. (T.C. November, 1668.) Licensed August 25, 1668. 4to. 1669. Actually published late in 1668. Not acted.

STROUDE, ——.
All-Plot ; or, The Disguises. Not printed. Mentioned by Downes as having been acted at Lincoln's Inn Fields between 1662 and 1671.

T

TALBOT, J.
Troas. A Tragedy. 4to. 1686. Unacted. A Translation from Seneca.

TATE, NAHUM. *Poet Laureate* (1652–1715).
Brutus Of Alba : Or, The Enchanted Lovers. A Tragedy D.G. June, 1678. 4to. 1678. (T.C. 6 Dec., 1678.) Licensed July 15, 1678.
The Loyal General. A Tragedy. D.G. the last week in November, 1679. 4to. 1680. (T.C. Feb., 1680.)

The History Of King Lear. Reviv'd with Alterations.
D.G. September, 1680. 4to. 1681. (T.C. May, 1681.)
4tos, 1689, 1703; 12mo, 1749, 1767.   Edited by Montague
Summers in *Shakespearean Adaptations*, 1922.

*The History Of King Richard The Second, Acted at the
Theatre Royal Under the Name of the Sicilian Usurper.* D.L.
12 December, 1680. 4to, 1681, for R. and J. Tonson,
"With a Prefatory *Epistle* in Vindication of the Author.
Occasion'd by the Prohibition of this *Play* on the Stage."
(T.C. June, 1681.) 4to, 1691, for James Knapton, as
"*The Sicilian Usurper :* A Tragedy, As it was Acted at the
Theatre Royal. With a Prefatory Epistle in Vindication
of the Author, occasioned by the Prohibition of this Play
on the Stage." This issue consists of the sheets of the 4to,
1681, with new title-page, and in the place of the sheet
carrying the Song *recto* and Persons Names *verso* (with
Tonson's advertisement) a new sheet carrying both *recto*
and *verso* an advertisement of Knapton.

*The Ingratitude Of A Common-Wealth : Or, the Fall of
Caius Martius Coriolanus.* D.L. November-December, 1681.
4to. 1682. (T.C. February, 1682.)

A Duke and no Duke. A Farce. D.L. 3 November, 1684.
4to. 1685. "With The several *Songs* set to Music, With
thorow Basses for the *Theorbo*, or *Basse* Viol." (T.C. Nov.,
1684.) 4to, 1693. "To which is now added, A Preface
concerning *Farce ;* With an Account of the *Personæ* and
Larvae, &c. Of the Ancient Theatre." (T.C. May,
1693.)

Cuckolds-Haven : Or, An Alderman No Conjurer. A Farce.
D.G. last week in June, 1685. Licensed August 14, 1685.
4to. 1685. (T.C. Nov., 1685.)

*The Island-Princess : (The Island Princess : Or, Generous
Portugals)* : As it is Acted At The Theatre Royal, Reviv'd

with Alterations. D.L. April, 1687. 4to. 1687. (T.C. June, 1687.)

Dido and Æneas. An Opera. " Perform'd at Mr. Josias Priest's Boarding-School at *Chelsey*, By Young Gentlewomen. The Words made by Mr. Nah. Tate, The Musick Composed by Mr. Henry Purcell." 1689. Epilogue in D'Urfey's *New Poems*, 1690 (p. 82). First printed, 1841, as edited by Sir George Macfarren for the Musical Antiquarian Society.

Injur'd Love : Or, The Cruel Husband. A Tragedy. Design'd to be Acted at the *Theatre Royal.* 4to. 1707. (T.C. July, 1707.)

TATHAM, JOHN.

The Fancies Theatre. 8vo. 1640. Contains in this collection, with separate title page,

    Love Crownes the End. A Pastorall Presented by the Schollees [*sic*] of Bingham in the County of Notingham ; in the yeare 1632. 1640.

The Mirrour of Fancies. With a Tragi-Comedy, intitled *Love Crownes the End.* Acted by the Schollars of Bingham in the County of Nottingham. 1657. (Another edition.)

The Distracted State, A Tragedy. Written in the Year 1641. Unacted. 4to. 1652.

The Scots Figgaries : or, A Knot of Knaves. A Comedy. Unacted. 4to. 1652.

The Rump : Or The Mirrour of The Late Times. A New Comedy. " Acted Many Times with Great Applause At the Private House in Dorset Court." Dorset Court, June, 1660. 4to. 1660. The Second Impression, Newly Corrected, with Additions. 4to. 1661.

The Dramatic Works of John Tatham. Edinburgh. 1879. Maidment and Logan.

THOMSON, THOMAS.

The Life of Mother Shipton. A New Comedy. As it was Acted Nineteen days together with great Applause. Written by T. T., n. d. [1661 ?]. The Bodleian copy has T. T[hompson], added in an old hand. Jolly's company; Cockpit or Salisbury Court.

The English Rogue. A New Comedy. As it was acted before several Persons of Honour with great Applause. Written by T. T. Licensed according to Order. 4to. 1668. Bodleian copy, T. T[hompson] added in an old hand. Jolly's company; Cockpit or Salisbury Court.

TROTTER, *Mrs.* CATHERINE (married Patrick Cockburn in 1708) (1679–1749).

Agnes de Castro, A Tragedy. D.L. November, 1695. 4to. 1696. Written by a Young Lady. (T.C. Hilary, Feb., 1696.)

Fatal Friendship. A Tragedy. L.I.F. 1698. 4to. 1698.

Love at a Loss, Or, Most Votes carry it. A Comedy. D.L. 23rd November, 1700. 4to. 1701. (Published 3 May, 1701. *Post Boy.*)

The Unhappy Penitent. A Tragedy. D.L. 4 February, 1700–1701. 4to. 1701. (2 August, 1701, *Post Man.*)

The Revolution Of Sweden. A Tragedy. Haymarket 11th February, 1706. Acted 6 times. 4to. 1706. (T.C. Easter, May, 1706.)

TUKE, RICHARD.

The Divine Comedian Or The Right Use Of Plays, Improved in a sacred Tragy-Comædy. Unacted. 4to. 1672. Not designed for the stage.

The Souls Warfare. A morality with *Empirea*, the Soul; *Cosmus*, the World; *Satan; Lust; Caro*, the Flesh;

Scandal, Poverty, Sickness; the three Theological Graces, and the Five Senses among the Dramatis Personæ.

TUKE, *Sir* SAMUEL (?–1674).
 The Adventures Of Five Hours. A Tragi-Comedy. Lincoln's Inn Fields, Thursday, 8 January, 1662–3. Folio, 1663. (*Febr.* 21°, 1662. Imprimatur *John Berkenhead.*) 4to, 1664, " The Second Edition "; 4to, 1671, " The Adventures Of Five Houres : . . . The Third Impression, Revis'd and Corrected by the Author Sir *Samuel Tuke* Kt. and Bar." 4to. 1704. This popular play was included in Dodsley, vol. XII, 1744; vol. XII, 1780; in Collier, vol. XII, 1827; in Hazlitt's *Dodsley*, vol. XV, 1876; and reprinted separately, with an Introduction by the present writer, 1928.

U

UNDERHILL, CAVE (1634–1710).
 Win her and Take Her, Or Old Fools will be Medling. A Comedy. D.L. 1691. 4to. 1691. This comedy is attributed by Anthony à Wood (*Athenæ Oxonienses*, ed. Bliss, 1820, Vol. IV, p. 601) to John Smythe (1662–?), an usher of Magdalen School, Oxford, who proceeded M.A. in 1686. D'Urfey's Epilogue, however, clearly names Underhill as the author, and Wood's statement is hardly reliable.

V

VANBRUGH, *Sir* JOHN (1664–1726).
 The Relapse; Or, Virtue in Danger. Being the Sequel of *The Fool in Fashion,* A Comedy. D.L. 21st November, 1696. 4to. 1697. (T.C. May, 1697, but issued in December, 1696.) S.R. 21 September, 1697. 4to, 1698; 4to, 1708; 12mo, 1727; 8vo, 1777.

Æsop. Part I, D.L. December, 1696; Part II, D.L. March, 1697. Part I (First Edition), 4to, 1697; Part II (First Edition), 4to, 1697. " The Second Edition, With the Addition of a Second Part,"4to, 1697; 4to, 1702; 12mo, 1730.

The Provok'd Wife : A Comedy. L.I.F. May, 1697. 4to. 1697. (T.C. May, 1697.) 4tos, 1698; 8vos, 1709, 1710; 12mo, 1727; 12mo, 1734; 12mo, Dublin, 1743, with certain scenes re-written. (Sir John Brute dons the dress of a woman of quality in place of a parson's gown.) 8vo. 1777. Dicks, 72.

The Pilgrim, A Comedy : As it is Acted at the *Theatre-Royal,* in Drury-Lane. *Written Originally by Mr.* Fletcher *and now very much Alter'd, with several Additions.* Likewise *A* Prologue, Epilogue, Dialogue *and* Masque. *Written by the late Great Poet Mr.* Dryden, *just before his Death, being the last of his Works.* D.L. 29 April, 1700. 4to. 1700 (anon.). Published 18th June, 1700. (*Post Man* and *London Gazette.*)

The False Friend : A Comedy. D.L. January, 1702. 4to. 1702 (anon.). Published 10th February, 1702. (*Post Man.*) 12mo, 1735 ; 8vo, 1777.

The Country House. A Farce. D.L. 23rd January, 1703. 8vo, 1715 ; 12mo, 1719; 8vo, 1725 (Dublin). *La Maison Rustique, or, The Country House.* 12mo. 1740.

Monsieur De Pourceaugnac Or Squire Trelooby. L.I.F. 30th March, 1704. 4to, 1704. Act I by Congreve ; Vanbrugh and Walsh adapted the Second and Third Acts.

The Confederacy : A Comedy. Haymarket, 30th October, 1705. 4to, 1705 ; 8vo, 1777. Often acted, and sometimes printed as *The City Wives Confederacy.* Dicks 170.

The Mistake : A Comedy. Haymarket, 27th December, 1705. 4to, 1706 ; 8vo, 1777.

The Cuckold in Conceit. A Farce. Haymarket 22nd March, 1707. Not Printed.

A Journey To London. Being Part of a Comedy Written by the Late Sir *John Vanbrugh*, Knt. And Printed after his own Copy : which (since his Decease) has been made an Intire Play, By Mr. *Cibber*. And call'd *The* Provok'd Husband, *&c.* 8vo, 1728 ; 12mo, 1734.

In some old catalogues a play called *The Cornish Squire* is attributed to Vanbrugh. This farce was brought upon the stage by James Ralph, and published, 8vo, 1734. He asserts that it was the original MS. of Congreve, Vanbrugh, and Walsh, and the original *Squire Trelooby*, for which see under CONGREVE, p. 43 ; and p. 122.

The Provok'd Wife, *The Confederacy*, and *The Mistake*, the three principal plays of Vanbrugh to keep the stage, were included in all the eighteenth-century (and later) editions, but where the texts are regulated from the prompt-books they are not entirely reliable.

Plays, Written by Sir John Vanbrugh, 2 vols., 12mo, 1730, 1735 ; 8vo, 1759 ; 12mo, 1765 (Dublin) ; 8vo, 1776. Vanbrugh's plays were reprinted with Wycherley, Congreve and Farquhar, introduction by Leigh Hunt, one volume, 8vo, 1840 ; reprinted 1849, 1851, 1864.

The Works of Sir John Vanbrugh. Edited by W. C. Ward. Two Volumes. Demy 8vo. 1893.

The Complete Works of Sir John Vanbrugh. Edited by Bonamy Dobrée and Geoffrey Webb. Four Volumes. 4to. 1927.

VILLIERS, GEORGE, *Duke of* BUCKINGHAM (1625–1687).

The Chances. A Comedy. D.L. February, 1666–7. (Seen by Pepys 5th February.) 4to, 1682 ; 4tos, 1692, 1705 ; 12mo, 1709, 1718 ; 8vo, 1723 ; 8vo, 1777 ; and in the various collected editions of Buckingham's Works. As altered by Garrick, 8vo, 1773. Dicks, No. 172. Garrick's version is given in R. Cumberland's *The British Drama*, Vol. III, 1817.

The Rehearsal. D.L. 7th December, 1671. S.R. 19th June, 1672. 4to, 1672 (T.C. 24th June, 1672); 4to, 1673; 4to, 1675, " The Third Edition with amendments and large Additions by the Author." 4tos, 1683, 1687, 1692, 1701; 12mo, 1709, " With a Key "; 8vo, 1710; 4to, 1711, " The Eighth Edition "; 12mo, 1718, " The Ninth Edition "; 8vo, 1723; 8vo, 1725 (Dublin); 12mo, 1734, " The Twelfth Edition "; 12mo, 1735, " The Thirteenth Edition "; 12mo, 1735 (Dublin); 12mo, 1739, as " The Twelfth Edition "; 8vo, 1755; 8vo, 1760, as " The Sixteenth Edition "; 12mo, 1768, " The Seventeenth Edition "; 8vo, 1774 (Edinburgh); 8vo, 1777; 8vo, 1787.

The Rehearsal is also included in the various editions of Buckingham's *Collected Works*, 8vo, 1704, 1715; 12mo, 1754; 8vo, 1775; as also in *A Collection of the Best British Plays*, 12mo, 1711, vol. IV. In Bell's *British Theatre*, vol. XXIX, 8vo, 1797. Edited by Montague Summers, 4to, 1914.

Sprat, Clifford, Butler, and even Waller and Cowley, are said to have contributed to *The Rehearsal*.

The Battle : Or The Rehearsal At White-Hall. A Farce. Unacted. In Buckingham's *Miscellaneous Works*, 8vo, 1704. Also termed " the Farce upon *Segmoor* Fight," and in the *Works*, 8vo, 1715, " The Battle of *Sedgmoor* Betwixt King *James*'s Forces And the Duke of Monmouth, Rehears'd at *Whitehall*. A Farce." With separate title-page, 8vo, 1714.

The Militant Couple : Or The Husband may thank himself. Unacted. In the *Works*, 8vo, 1704.

The Belgic Heroe Unmasked : Or The Deliverer set forth in his proper Colours. Unacted. In the *Works*, 8vo, 1704.

The Restauration : Or Right will take Place. A Tragi-comedy. Probably Unacted. " From the Original Copy, never before Printed," 8vo, 1714. In the *Works,* 8vo, General title-page, 1715, " The Third Edition."

WALKER, WILLIAM (1679–1726).
Victorious Love. A Tragedy. D.L. June, 1698. 4to. 1698.
Marry, or do Worse. A Comedy. L.I.F. 1 November, 1703. 4to. 1704 (anon.).

WALLER, EDMUND (1606–1687).
Pompey The Great. A Tragedy. As it was Acted by the Servants of His Royal Highness the Duke of York. Translated out of French by Certain Persons Of Honour. L.I.F. December, 1663. Also acted at Whitehall. 4to. 1664. Waller translated the First Act of this play from Corneille's *La Mort de Pompée.* See also under Sir EDWARD FILMER, SIDNEY GODOLPHIN, CHARLES SACKVILLE, and Sir CHARLES SEDLEY, who translated severally the remaining four acts.
The Second Part of Mr. Waller's Poems. Containing His Alteration of the Maids Tragedy. Printed for Tho. Bennet. 8vo. 1690.
The Maid's Tragedy Altered. With some other Pieces By Edmund Waller, Esq ; Not before Printed. Printed for Jacob Tonson. 8vo. 1690. These two alterations differ, and it seems probable that the Tonson edition represents a revised version of the changes.

WESTON, JOHN.
The Amazonian Queen ; Or, The Amours Of Thalestris To Alexander the Great. A Tragi-Comedy. Unacted. Licensed Feb. 11, 1666–7. 4to. 1667.

WHARTON, *Lady* ANNE née LEE (1632 ?–1685).
Love's Martyr, or Witt above Crowns. A Tragedy. Unacted, and not printed. British Museum, Add. MS. 28693.
The subject of this piece, which is written in blank verse,
is the love of Ovid for Julia, daughter of Augustus Cæsar.

WHITAKER, WILLIAM.
The Conspiracy Or The Change Of Government. A Tragedy.
D.G. March, 1680. 4to. 1680.

WILD, *Dr.* ROBERT (1609–1679).
The Benefice. A Comedy. "By R.*W*. D.D. Author of
Iter Boreale. Written in his Younger Days : Now made
Publick for promoting Innocent Mirth. Licensed and
Enter'd." Unacted. 4to. 1689. An imperfect copy,
MS. (*c*. 1641 ?), is preserved in the British Museum, MS.
Lansd. 807.

WILLIAMS, JOSEPH.
Have at all, or the Midnight Adventures. D.L. April, 1694.
Not Printed.   *The Gentleman's Journal*, May, 1694 (III, 134).

WILMOT, JOHN, *Earl of* ROCHESTER (1647–1680).
Lucina's Rape Or The Tragedy of Vallentinian. D.L. 1678,
(at latest before June, 1679). Not Printed. British Museum,
Add. MSS. 28692, ff. 3a–69a.
Valentinian : A Tragedy. *Lucina's Rape* with some
variants. D.L. 20 February, 1683–4. 4to, 1685, " As 'tis
Alter'd by the late Earl of Rochester, And Acted at the
Theatre-Royal." (T.C. Nov., 1684.) *Valentinian* is included
in several editions of Rochester's *Poems* ; 8vo, 1691, 1696,
1705, 1709, 1710 ; 12mo, 1714 ; 8vo, 1732.
Sodom. A Play. Probably unacted. 8vo, Antwerp
[London], 1684 ; 12mo, Paris, 1904, " mit einer Einleitung

von L. S. A. M. v. Römer." This issue also appeared in Vol. IX of *Kruptadia*, Heilbronn et Paris, 1911. Another edition, 8vo, n.d. (1930). There are at least four extant MSS. of *Sodom*. (*a*) British Museum, Harleian MSS. 7312, as " Sodom or The Quintessence of Debauchery By E of R." (*b*) Victoria and Albert Museum, South Kensington, Dyce Library, Dyce MS. 43. (*c*) Hamburger Staats-und Universitätsbibliothek ; " Sodom A Play By The Earl of Rochester. . . . Antwerp Printed in the Year 1684," a quarto, bound with MS., *Beverlandi Otia Oxoniensis*, from the library of the Frankfort bibliographer, Z. C. von Uffenbach. (*d*) The Hague Library. There were two MS. translations of *Sodom* in the Soleinne library. " *Le Roi de Sodome*, Tragédie en prose, en 5 actes, par le Comte de Rochester, en 1658 [*sic*] traduit de l'anglais, par M****, 1744." 4to. Said to be the work of Bussy-Rabutin. " *Sodome*, comédie en 5 actes et en prose, par le Comte de Rochester, traduite de l'anglais, 1682." 8vo. Both these MSS. were destroyed. (See *Les Priapeia, Note de Lessing, Traduite par Philomneste Junior*, Bruxelles, 1866, p. 30, note. Also, *L'Intermédiaire des Chercheurs et Curieux*, *etc.*, vol. X, p. 348.)

L'Embrasement de Sodome, " comédie traduite de l'anglais sur un manuscrit du seizième siècle, 1740," 8vo, a MS. in the Soleinne Library, appears to be another piece, and to have nothing to do with Rochester. It has even been attributed to Voltaire. (*La Cauchoise, ou, Mémoires d'une courtisane célèbre*, a work earlier than 1788.) See Gay's *Bibliographie des Ouvrages relatifs a l'Amour, etc.*, 4e éd. Tome I, c. 501. The provenance of this MS. to-day is not known.

There is a German translation. *Earl of Rochester. Sodom. Ein Spiel.* Folio, Leipzig, 1909. Translated by Theophil

Marquardt. This also appeared in Vol. XIV of *Bibliotheca Erotica et Curiosa*, 8vo, n.d.

A Scene of Sr Robert Hoard's Play, written by The Earl of Rochester. British Museum, Add. MSS. 28692, ff. 70a–75b. A fragment of 263 verses. Designed to be inserted in a play, *The Conquest of China by the Tartars*, composed by Sir Robert Howard, and not printed. In September, 1697, Dryden writes, in a letter to his two sons at Rome, that he proposes to alter and produce this piece, but he abandoned the project.

La Cauchoise mentions "Fragment d'une comédie en prose des même auteur [Rochester] et traducteur [Bussy-Rabutin]." This, however, is almost certainly fictitious, or an error for some other piece.

Collected Works of John Wilmot Earl of Rochester, Edited by John Hayward. 1926. Includes *Valentinian,* pp. 161–238 ; and *A Scene of Sir Robert Howard's Play,* pp. 239–247.

WILSON, JOHN (1627–1696).
The Cheats : A Comedy. T.R., Vere Street, about 20 March, 1662–3. (S.R. 9 Nov., 1663.) 4to. 1664. " Written in the Year M.DC.LXII." *Imprimatur,* Nov. 5, 1663. 4to, 1671 ; 1684 ; 1693, " with the addition of a new Song." A MS. of *The Cheats,* with passages deleted, and thus licensed for representation by Herbert, is preserved in the Library of Worcester College, Oxford. Edited by M. G. Nahm, 1935.
Andronicus Commenius. A Tragedy. Unacted. 4to. 1664. Imprimatur, January 18, 1663–4. Preface dated 15 January, 1663.
The Projectors. A Comedy. Possibly not acted. (S.R., *The Projector,* 15 Feb., 1664–5.) 4to. 1665. *Imprimatur* Jan. 13, 1664.

Belphegor : Or The Marriage of the Devil. A Tragi-Comedy. D. G. late in June, 1690. 4to. 1691. Licensed October 13, 1690. (T.C. Feb., 1691.) There are copies of the 4to, 1691, with slightly varying title-pages. The Author's original MS. of *Belphegor*, 86 folio sheets, was described in a catalogue of Messrs. Pickering and Chatto (about 1910) ; and is now, I understand, preserved in an American private library. A note said : " This MS. bears all the evidence of having been used for the prompter's copy for more than one production."
The Dramatic Works of John Wilson. Edinburgh. 1874. Maidment and Logan.

WRIGHT, JAMES.
Le Malade Imaginaire, " A Comedy of Moliere, translated out of French." Not Printed. The translator's holograph MS., 42 pp., is extant.

WRIGHT, JOHN.
Thyestes. A Tragedy, Translated out of Seneca. To which is Added *Mock-Thyestes,* In Burlesque. Unacted. 8vo. 1674.

WRIGHT, THOMAS.
The Female Vertuoso's. A Comedy. D.G. April, 1693 4to. 1693. (T.C. Nov., 1693.) 8vo, 1721, as *No Fools Like Wits ; Or, The Female Vertuosoes.* This second edition was reprinted by Curll when the comedy was revived at L.I.F. on 10 January, 1721, and played for three nights that season, in opposition to Colley Cibber's *The Refusal ; or, The Ladies Philosophy,* produced at D.L. on 14 February, 1720–1, since both plays are founded on Molière's *Les Femmes Savantes.*

WYCHERLEY, WILLIAM (1640–1715).
Love in a Wood, Or St James's Park. A Comedy. D.L.
April, 1671. (S.R. 6 Oct., 1671.) 4to, 1672. (T.C. 20
Nov., 1671.) 4to, 1693, 1694, 1711 ; 8vo. 1776.
The Gentleman Dancing-Master. A Comedy. D.G.
February-March, 1671-2. (S.R. 18 Sept., 1672.) 4to,
1673. (T.C. 21 Nov., 1672.) 4to, 1693, 1702 ; 8vo, 1777.
The Country-Wife. A Comedy. D.L. January, 1674-5.
(S.R. 13 Jan. 1674-5.) 4to, 1675. (T.C. 10 May, 1675.)
4to, 1683, 1688, 1695. Dublin, 12mo, 1733 ; 8vo, 1777. In
some late eighteenth century reprints under the title of
The Country-Wife is given Garrick's *The Country Girl.* See,
for example, *The New English Theatre,* Vol. XI ; 1777.
Garrick's adaptation of *The Country-Wife* as *The Country
Girl* was printed 8vo, 1766.
The Plain-Dealer. A Comedy. D.L. December, 1676.
4to, 1677. (T.C. 28 May, 1677.) 4to, 1677, " The Second
Edition " ; (T.C. 26 Nov., 1677.) 4to, 1677, " The Third
Edition." 4to, 1678 ; 1681. 4to, 1686 as " The Fourth
Edition." 4to, 1691 (T.C. Nov., 1691.) 4to, 1694 as " The
Sixth Edition " (T.C. June, 1694). 4to, 1700 (T.C. Feb.,
1701, as " The Sixth Edition "). 4to, 1709 ; 12mo, 1727 ;
12mo, 1735 ; 8vo, 1777.
Wycherley's four comedies were collected in one volume,
8vo, 1713, as " The Works of the ingenious Mr. William
Wycherley." Each play has a separate title dated 1712.
Other collected editions of the four comedies are : 12mo,
1729 ; 12mo, 1735, *Plays Written by Mr. Wm. Wycherley,*
each play having separate pagination ; 8vo, 1768. Wycherley's Comedies were reprinted in 1840 with the Dramatic
Works of Congreve, Vanbrugh, and Farquhar, in one
volume, 8vo, 1840, with a critical and biographical introduction by Leigh Hunt ; reprinted, 1849, 1851, 1866. The

four comedies are included in the Mermaid Series, 1888, with an Introduction by W. C. Ward.

The Complete Works of William Wycherley, edited by Montague Summers.   4 vols., 1924.

The dates of the original productions of Wycherley's comedies are difficult to determine, and considerable internal as well as somewhat external evidence has to be sifted and weighed.   The suggestions, as above, which I have made for *The Gentleman Dancing-Master, The Country Wife*, and *The Plain-Dealer*, have been adopted by Mr. J. R. A. Nicoll, Mr. W. Connely, and others.   *Love in a Wood*, which I assigned to October, 1671, I have now put back to the spring of that year, although I confess I doubt whether the early autumn might not after all prove to be the more correct.

ADDENDA

In a letter to *The Times Literary Supplement*, 4th October, 1934, Mr. B. M. Wagner, of Georgetown University, Washington, has drawn attention to the following MSS. of seventeenth-century plays :

BIRKHEAD, HENRY (1617–1696).
  The Female Rebellion, A Tragicomedy. Autograph MS., Tanner 466, Bodleian Library.
  Printed (with variations) by Alexander Smith, 1872, with notes by J. P. Collier, from MS. 635, Hunterian Museum, Glasgow.
  See, however, a subsequent letter from Mr. Alfred Harbage of the University of Pennsylvania, *The Times Literary Supplement*, 8th November, 1934. Mr. Harbage suggests that *The Female Rebellion* may rather be the work of the author of *Cola's Fury ; or, Lirenda's Misery*, 4to, 1645, one Henry Burkhead, a Bristol merchant, concerning whom nothing further seems known.

CARLIELL, LODOWICK (1602–1675).
  Arviragus and Philicia. MS. Eng. misc. d. 11, Bodleian ; and a MS. with the author's signature in the library of Lord Leconfield, Petworth House : *Hist. MSS. Com.*, 6th rep., 1877, 312.

DAVENANT, *Sir* WILLIAM, *Poet Laureate* (1606–1668).
   The Siege of Rhodes. MS. 787. 4o (Fol. 287). "William Davenant's the Siege of Rhode."—1694 et 1695. The Public Library of Douai.

DRYDEN, JOHN, *Poet Laureate* (1631–1700).
   The Indian Emperour, Or, The Conquest Of Mexico By The Spaniards. MS. 787. 3o (Fol. 252). "John Dryden's the Indian emperor." The Public Library of Douai.

LEE, NATHANIEL (1649–1692).
   Mithridates King of Pontus : A Tragedy. MS. 787. 2° (Fol. 210). "Nat Lee's Mithradates, king of Pontus." The Public Library of Douai.

MANUCHE, *Major* COSMO (–1665 ?).
   The Just General. A Tragicomedy. 4to. 1650.
   The Loyal Lovers. A Tragicomedy. 4to. 1652.
   The Bastard. A Tragedy. 4to. 1652. (Attributed by Edward Archer, 1656.)

The following MS. plays by this author are preserved in the Earl of Northampton's library at Castle Ashby :
   The Banished Shepherdesse. A second MS. is in the Huntington Library, California.
   The Feast. A Comedy. A second MS. is in the Library of Worcester College, Oxford.
   The Mandrake. A Comedy. (Unfinished.)
   Agamemmnnon. A Tragedy. (Unfinished.)
   Lenotius, K. of Ciprus. A Tragedy.
   The Captives. A Comedy. (Unfinished.)
   Mariamni. A Tragedy.
   A Tragedy without a title.
   A Comedy without a title.

In *The Feast* there are allusions to Tuke's *The Adventures of Five Hours*, and Dryden and Howard's *The Indian-Queen*.

In a letter to *The Times Literary Supplement*, 18th October, 1934, Miss Ethel Seaton has drawn attention to the Diary of two Dutch visitors to London, who, under the date 1st February, 1661–62 (Old Style, 22nd January, 1661–62), record that they saw at the Red Bull a Comedy *Den nieuw-gemaakten Adelman* (*The New-Made Nobleman*).

So far as I am aware no serious attempt has been made to identify this play, and, having regard to the lack of further details, conjecture would seem to be singularly fruitless. It is, of course, possible that it was the revival of some older piece which has been entirely lost.

In a letter to *The Times Literary Supplement*, 15th November, 1934, Mr. A. Watkin-Jones has drawn attention to an unprinted Masque by Major Samuel Holland, *The Enchanted Grove*, in Two Parts, 4to MS., preserved in the library at Castle Ashby.

Holland wrote a Masque, *Venus and Adonis*, which is printed in *Wit and Fancy in a Maze ; or, The incomparable Champion of Love and Beautie*, 12mo, 1656; and hence appeared in *Romancio-Mastix ; or, A Romance on Romances*, 12mo, 1660.

The Enchanted Grove is dedicated to James, Earl of Northampton ; and Bishop Percy is doubtless correct when he noted : " I suppose this Major Holland (as well as Cosmo Manuche) was an Officer in the Regiment raised by the s^d Earl of Northampton in the Cause of Kg. Charles I."

P. 14. *Love will finde out the Way, An Excellent Comedy By T. B. As it was acted with great Applause, by her Majesties Servants, at the Phœnix in Drury Lane.* 4to. 1661.

This is none other than Shirley's *The Constant Maid,*

first printed, 4to, 1640. T. B. furnishes an epilogue of half-a-dozen lines. The quarto 1661 was re-issued in 1667 with a new title-page, *The Constant Maid : or, Love will finde out the Way. A Comedy, By J. S. As it is now Acted at the new Playhouse called the Nursery, in Hatton-Garden.*

P. 14. *Honour in the End.* A Comedy. Advertised at the end of *Wit and Drollery*, 12mo, 1661. This piece, no doubt an older play, apparently was not published. The same may be said of *The Fool Transformed*, a Comedy similarly advertised.

P. 14. *The Dancing Master.* Pepys, 21st May, 1662, saw *The French Dancing Master*, i.e. *The Varietie*, with Lacy as Galliard. There is also a droll of this name from *The Varietie*, but here the comedy itself is intended.

P. 14. *The French Schoolmaster.* A Comedy. 4to. Advertised at the end of *The Wits*, 8vo, 1662, as sold by Henry Marsh, at the Princes Arms, in Chancery Lane.

P. 14. *The Labyrinth.* Add : Pepys describes *The Labyrinth* as a poor play, " there being nothing in it but the odd accidents that fell out, by a lady's being bred up in man's apparel, and a man in a woman's." *The Labyrinth*, 8vo, 1795, is a version by the Rev. M. Stratford of Thomas Corneille's *Ariane.*

P. 14. *Noah's Flood.* A licence to act a play of this name, with other scenes, throughout the country was issued on 14th April, 1662, to George Bayley, the manager of a company of eight.

P. 15. *Merry Andrew.* " To Bartholomew Fair, and there did see a ridiculous, obscene little stage-play, called " Marry Andrey," a foolish thing, but seen by every body." Pepys, 29th August, 1668.

P. 15. *The Imperial Tragedy.* Langbaine, *English Dramatick Poets*, Oxford, 1691, p. 535, notes, This Play " has been acted (if I mistake not) at the Nursery in *Barbican.*" The Latin play from which it was taken is named *Zeno.*

P. 16. *The Rival Mother.* A Comedy. 8vo. 1678.

P. 17. *The Perjur'd Nun,* 4to, 1680, as acted at the Theatre Royal, is merely a reprint of Anthony Brewer's *The Love-sick King, An English Tragical History ; With the Life and Death of Cartesmunda, the Fair Nun of Winchester.* 4to. 1655.

P. 17. *An Evening Adventure ; or, A Night's Intrigue.* Comedy from the Spanish. Anon. 1680. Identified by the *Biographia Dramatica,* 1812, Vol. II, p. 203, with *An Evening's Intrigue.* A Comedy translated from the Spanish ; and the scene removed into England by Capt. John Stevens. 8vo. 1707. Printed in a book called *The Spanish Libertines.*

P. 17. *The Muse of New-Market. The Merry Milkmaid of Islington* is from Nabbes' *Totenham-Court.*

P. 17. *Fools have Fortune, or Luck's all.* J. Payne Collier, in his " History of the Restoration Stage " (unpublished MS. now preserved in the Theatre section of the Harvard University Library), Part II, p. 202, says that Charlotte Butler made her first appearance in a comedy of this name. There does not appear to be any mention of the play elsewhere, and many of Collier's statements are more than suspect. If *Fools have Fortune* is a genuine piece, and such may well be the case, it must be dated 1680.

P. 20. *Poeta Infamis ; or A Poet not worth hanging.* 4to. 1692. Not intended for the stage. A dialogue satirizing D'Urfey.

P. 20. *The Puritanical Justice ; or, The Beggars turn'd Thieves.* By way of Farce, as it was lately Acted in and about the City of *London.* 4to. 1698. A satire upon Sir Humphrey Edwin (1642–1707), who was Lord Mayor of London in 1697, and who incurred much odium during his term of office.

P. 40.   CLARKE, TIMOTHY, M.D., F.R.C.P. (?–1672).

"Dr. Clerke fell to reading a new play, newly writ, of a friend's of his ; but, by his discourse and confession afterwards, it was his own." Pepys, *Diary*, 13th February, 1666–67.

P. 45.   COWLEY, ABRAHAM (1618–1667).   Add : *Naufragium Joculare*, 12mo, 1638 : " A Latine Comedy call'd *Naufargium Joculare*, which was acted before the University of *Cambridge* by the Members of *Trinity* Colledge, the second day of *February*, 1638." Langbaine, *op. cit.*, p. 86.

P. 52.   DAVENANT, *Sir* WILLIAM, *Poet Laureate* (1606–1668).   Add : On Thursday, 10th December, 1663, Pepys heard news " of a rare play to be acted this week of Sir William Davenant's : the story of Henry the Eighth with all his wives." In the third week of December, 1663, *Henry VIII* was produced at Lincoln's Inn Fields with much splendour, but it does not appear that Davenant made any material alteration in or addition to Shakespeare's and Fletcher's scenes.   See Downes, *Roscius Anglicanus*, ed. Montague Summers, pp. 24 and 183–4.   Also *Shakespeare Adaptations*, 1922, ed. Montague Summers, Introduction, pp. xxxvi–xxxix.

P. 55.   DOGGETT, THOMAS (?–1721).   Add : *Mad Tom of Bedlam ; or, The Distressed Lovers ; with the Comical Humours of Squire Numskull*. N.P. A Droll, acted at Bartholomew and Southwark Fairs.

" At Parker's and Doggett's Booth, near Hosier Lane end, in Smithfield during the time of Bartholomew Fair, will be presented a New Droll, called *Fryar Bacon ; or, The Country Justice*. With the Humours of *Tolfree*, the Miller, and his Son *Ralph*, acted by Mr. *Doggett*. With Variety of

Scenes, Machines, Songs, and Dances. *Vivat Rex*." 1691.
This Droll, *Fryar Bacon*, was not printed.

P. 55. DOMVILLE, *alias* TAYLOR, SILAS (1624–1678).
The Serenade, or Disappointment. N.P., but possibly acted
at D.L., 1669–1670. See Pepys, 7 May, 1669.

P. 61. DRYDEN, JOHN, *Poet Laureate* (1631–1700). The
Dryden folios (*Jacob Tonson*), 1701, are sometimes found
with general titles : *The Works Of the late Famous Mr. John
Dryden ;* and *The Works of Mr. John Dryden.*

P. 73. FLECKNOE, *The Rev. Fr.* RICHARD (?–1678 ?).
Add : The *Biographia Dramatica*, 1812, Vol. I, Part I, p. 781,
noticing *The Physician against His Will*, remarks : " The
editor of the new edition of Earle's *Microcosmography*, 1811,
p. 307, mentions a MS. note in his copy of Langbaine,
stating it to have been printed in 1712." It is almost certain
that there was no such edition of 1712, and indeed the same
work, *Biographia Dramatica*, 1812, Vol. III, p. 464, again
recording *The Physician against His Will*, more judiciously
observes, we do not believe " that it was ever printed."

P. 76. HEAD, RICHARD (1636 ?–1678).
Hic et Ubique ; or The Humours of Dublin. 4to. 1663.
Said to have been acted privately with great applause.

P. 77. HORNE, JOHN.
Fortune's Taske ; or, The Fickle Fair One. 1684. N.P.
John Horne, who was of New College, Oxford, M.A.,
30th June, 1677, left this MS. play at his death.

P. 77. HUGHES, JOHN (1677–1720).
Amalasont, Queen of the Goths. A Tragedy. Written in
1696. N.P. MS. formerly in possession of the Rev. John
Duncombe.

The Misanthrope. A translation from Molière. In the Second Number of *The Monthly Amusement,* 1709 ; and reprinted by Ozell in his version of Molière.

Calypso and Telemachus. An Opera. Queen's Theatre, Haymarket. 8vo. 1712 ; 12mo, 1735.

Apollo and Daphne. A Masque. D.L. Music by Pepusch. 4to. 1716.

Orestes. Unacted. From Euripides. 8vo, 1717; 12mo, 1735.

The Siege of Damascus. A Tragedy. D.L. 17th February, 1719–20. 8vo, 1720 ; and very many subsequent editions.

The Miser. From Molière, the first act only ; and *Cupid and Hymen,* a Pastoral Masque, were both first printed in the *Works,* 2 vols., 12mo, 1735.

Sophy Mirza. A Tragedy. N.P. Acts I and II were written by Hughes, who died before he had completed the play. It was finished by his brother-in-law, William Duncombe, in whose family the MS. remained.

P. 82. KILLIGREW, THOMAS (1612–1683). Add : *The Parsons Wedding,* although (in greater part, at least) written before 1642, was not produced until the 5th or 6th October, 1664, at the Theatre Royal, when it was " acted by nothing but women." See Pepys, *Diary,* 11th October, 1664.

Among the books representing Killigrew's works in the portrait frontispiece to the folio, 1664, is seen a piece named *The Revenge.* This may have been an alternative title (afterwards discarded) for one of his extant plays, or else it may be some drama which he contemplated but did not write.

P. 89. MEDBOURNE, MATTHEW (?–1679). Add : When *Every Man in His Humour* was revived by Killigrew's company, probably at D.L. about 1670–71, a new Epilogue "spoken by *Ben Johnson*'s Ghost" was written by the Earl of Dorset. See *Poems on Several Occasions*, 8vo, 1673, p. 29. In this address we have the following couplet :

> Here's Master *Matthew*, our domestic Wit,
> Does promise one o' th' ten Plays he has writ.

The town gull in Jonson's comedy, Master Matthew, is, of course, a poet and covers a whole realm of paper, but it may be that there is also in this Epilogue a satirical reflection upon Medbourne as a dramatist.   Langbaine, *op. cit.*, p. 366, praises Medbourne's "good parts," and it is not altogether unlikely that he was the author of several plays which have not come down to us.

P. 91.   MOTTEUX, PETER ANTHONY (1663–1718).   To *Acis and Galatea* add : It seems possible that this Masque by Motteux was introduced into an opera *The Mad Lover*, which was presumably based on Fletcher's play.   The Burney MS. records a performance at Lincoln's Inn Fields on 24th June, 1701 : "*Circe* and *Mad Lover* with the *Wedding Day*, by Mr. Doggett and Mr. Bowman." It is hardly conceivable that *The Mad Lover* should be an alternative title for *Acis and Galatea*.   See further A. C. Sprague, *Beaumont and Fletcher on the Restoration Stage*, 1926, Appendix I, pp. 271–73.

P. 100, R.   After R, and before RAVENSCROFT, insert : R., W., M.A.   *The Christmas Ordinary.*   A private Show, wherein is expressed the Jovial Freedom of that Festival. Acted at a Gentlemans House among other Revels.   4to. 1682.

The Christmas Ordinary.   Comedy by Trinity College, Oxford, was entered S.R. 29 June, 1660, but apparently not printed.

P. 103. RIVERS, S.J., *The Rev. Fr.* ANTONY (*alias* THOMAS BLEWETT).

The Traytor. " A Tragedy, with Alterations, Amendments, and Additions, as it is now Acted at the Theatre Royal," March, 1692. " Written by Mr. Rivers." 4to. 1692. (T.C. Easter, May, 1692). In the Dedication it is said that this Tragedy was written by Fr. Rivers, S.J., and, adds Genest, revised and improved by Shirley, under whose name it was licensed 4th May, 1631, acted " by Her Majesties Servants," and printed, 4to, 1635.

In *The Gentleman's Journal*, April, 1692, Motteux writes : " *The Traytor*, an old Tragedy, hath not only been revived the last Month, but also been reprinted with Alterations and Amendments ; It was supposed to be *Shirley*'s, but he only usher'd it in to the Stage ; The Author of it was one Mr. *Rivers*, a Jesuite." Fr. Antony Rivers was sometime secretary to Fr. Henry Garnett.

P. 111. SHADWELL, THOMAS, *Poet Laureate* (1641–1692). The Librarian to the Duke of Portland, Mr. F. R. W. Needham, informs me that there are preserved at Welbeck Abbey MSS. of *The Sullen Lovers : or, The Impertinents* and *The Humorists*, which present features of considerable interest. The corrections and additions seemingly can only have been made by the author, whilst the MS. of *The Humorists* supplies the text of this comedy in its original unexpurgated state " before the Sting was taken out," since Shadwell was compelled to modify the satire when it appeared upon the stage. See *The Complete Works of Thomas Shadwell*, 1927, ed. by Montague Summers, Vol. I, Introduction, pp. lxxvii–lxxviii, and lxxxii–lxxxv.

P. 119. TATE, NAHUM. *Poet Laureate* (1652–1715). The one really complete copy of Purcell's autograph score of *Dido and Æneas* is preserved in the library of S. Michael's College, Tenbury. For details see Professor E. J. Dent, *Foundations of English Opera*, 1928, pp. 178–180.

P. 122. VANBRUGH, *Sir* JOHN (1664–1726). Add under *The Pilgrim* : *The Secular Masque*. Written by Dryden, and set to music by Mr. Boyce. 8vo. 1745.

P. 130. WYCHERLEY, WILLIAM (1640–1715). John Lee's adaptation in two acts of *The Country-Wife*, D.L. 26 April, 1765, was printed as *The Country Wife*, 8vo, no date [1765]. Isaac Bickerstaffe's adaptation of *The Plain-Dealer*, D.L., December, 1765, was printed as *The Plain Dealer*, 8vo, 1766 ; and 1767. John Kemble's adaptation, *The Plain Dealer*, D.L., 27 February, 1796, was printed, 8vo, in that year.

Midnights Intrigues, a play acted at Dorset Garden in the spring of 1677; N.P. ; is mentioned in the Prologue to *Wits Led by the Nose*, for which see under CHAMBERLAYNE, p. 36.

PUPPET-PLAYS

Even during the Commonwealth puppet-plays were " still up with uncontrolled allowance," whilst at the Restoration their popularity, if possible, increased, and they were patronized and enjoyed by quality and mobile alike. The foreign puppet-plays were much followed, and Antonio Di Voto, a famous " punchenello," was licensed by Herbert as Master of a Puppet-Show. The native puppet-plays generally presented a scriptural subject or some semi-historical story. Thus *The Prodigal Son*, *The Court of King Solomon*, *Good Queen Esther*, *Patient Grissel*, and *Dick Whittington* remained prime favourites until late in the eighteenth century.

Pepys saw " an Italian puppet-play " on Saturday, 9th May, 1662, " within the rayles " at Covent Garden. In August, 1667, Lady Castlemaine was at " a puppet-play *Patient Grizill* " at Bartholomew Fair. " The puppet-show of *Whittington*," which Pepys found " pretty to see," proved a great attraction at Southwark Fair in September, 1668.

There are many other references in the *Diary* (and else where) to puppet-plays, which forty years after, under Powell the famous puppet-man, had become exceedingly elaborate and adroitly contrived.

Such other entertainments of a panoramic kind as " Para-dice, shown at Hatton-house in Holborn from 3 of the Clock to 8 every afternoon," *City Mercury*, 17–24 February, 1675, attracted large crowds in Restoration London.

The history of the puppet-play in England is full of interest, but since the " Words " of these little dramas were not printed, more than the briefest note would be out of place in *A Bibliography of the Restoration Drama*.